A Scripture Union resource boo

ULTIMATE
Quizzes

Richard and Mary Chewter

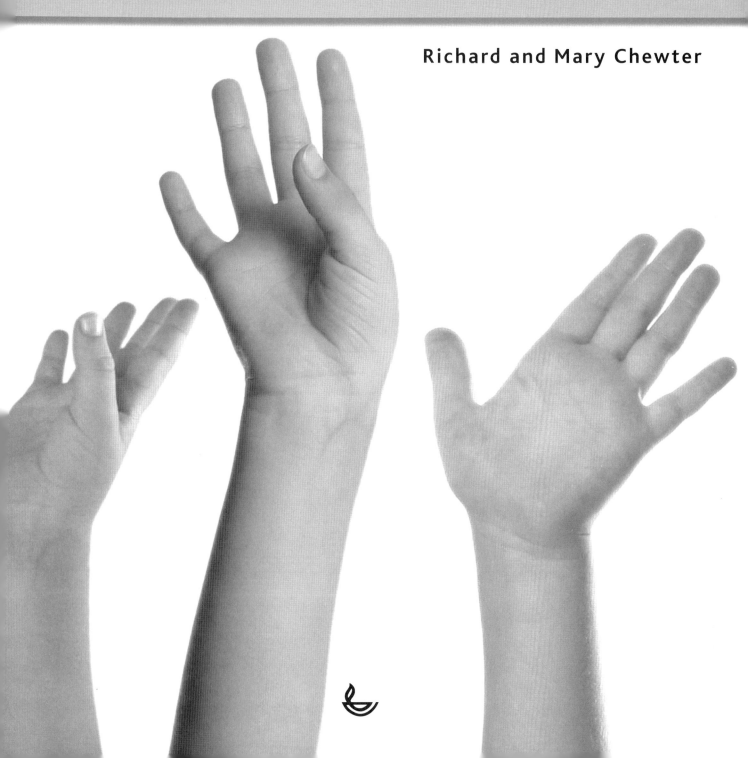

© Richard and Mary Chewter 2008
ISBN 978 1 84427 366 9
Scripture Union, 207–209 Queensway, Bletchley, Milton Keynes, MK2 2EB, England
Email: info@scriptureunion.org.uk
Website: www.scriptureunion.org.uk

Scripture Union Australia, Locked Bag 2, Central Coast Business Centre, NSW 2252, Australia
Website: www.scriptureunion.org.au

Scripture Union USA, PO Box 987, Valley Forge, PA 19482, USA
Website: www.scriptureunion.org

The material in this book was originally published as Quiz resource book

British Library Cataloguing-in-Publication Data.
A catalogue record of this book is available from the British Library.
Printed and bound in Singapore by Tien Wah Press Ltd
Cover design by Wild Associates
Internal layout by C. Michael Lorenz

Scripture Union is an international Christian charity working with churches in more than 130 countries, providing resources to bring the good news about Jesus to children, young people and families and encouraging them to develop spiritually through the Bible and prayer.

As well as our network of volunteers, staff and associates who run holidays, church-based events and school Christian groups, we produce a wide range of publications and support those who use our resources through training programmes.

ULTIMATE
Quizzes

Contents

* For titles of individual quiz presentation ideas and types of quiz questions, see index.

ULTIMATE Quizzes

Introduction

Our thanks to the following for their contributions:

Colin Draper
Helen Franklin
Andy Frith
Paul Godfrey
John Hattam
Steve Hutchinson
Vic Lanchester
Dai Lewis
John Marshall
Jeremy Moore
Kevin Moore
Frank Nelson
Margaret Owen
Andy Saunders
Colin Stephenson
Simon Ward

Reasons for using quizzes

You know the situation. You're at the Service Planning Meeting and, over coffee, some bright spark volunteers you for the quiz on Sunday. After all, it will fill out the service, won't it? A severe outbreak of panic grips you. Then you have a bright idea. You draw a grid on the board. 'Noughts and crosses!' you announce with enthusiasm. Infectious groaning spreads across the room.

You may have found yourself in a similar situation, struggling to think of something different to do as a quiz, either for an all-age service, or for one of the children's groups. Either way, ideas soon run out, and the repetition of a familiar quiz – 'noughts and crosses', for example – is the only way out. Well, if this sounds like you, then this book is for you.

It is not just a set of questions and answers, but a resource book of ideas, that will help you to present a quiz in an exciting and relevant way. All the quizzes are photocopiable. There are sections on how to use them with different age groups, how to improve presentation, and the use of materials and other resources.

Don't allow yourself to become 'stuck in a rut'. Part of the fun of using quizzes is to experiment and try new things.

Many of the quizzes have been used in services and missions that we are involved in. I guess it's true to say that this collection represents some of our favourites, and I would encourage you to use these tried and tested quizzes in your own groups.

'So why use quizzes at all? They're just time fillers.'

Comments like this are heard all the time. Used properly, quizzes can be part of many different activities, such as:

- All-age services
- Mid-week clubs
- Adult groups
- Sunday schools
- Missions

They can be an important part of your programme for the following reasons:

1. They can be used to liven up a club, activity or service.
2. We all learn through games. You only have to watch children playing to see how they learn about their world through their games. They can learn confidence in taking part in quizzes: quiet children who know the answer can be given a chance to take part, more confident children can be encouraged to take an active role. The same also applies to adults, of course!
3. They can be used to encourage children and adults to learn together.
4. Quizzes can introduce new ideas. They can be the basis of initial teaching.
5. Quizzes can be used to review previous teaching and to check on the teaching retained. They may also serve to check levels of understanding, and therefore allow adjustments to teaching agendas.
6. Quizzes are an excellent medium for breaking down barriers, allowing people to get to know one another in a fun, learning situation. They can be used as an ice-breaker at the beginning of an event. This can either be noisy or quiet.

As an example, a 'round the wall' quiz can be used to great effect. Ten pictures are placed around the room. A pencil, and paper marked one to ten, is given to each person. They then try to identify the pictures around the room. This can be used to introduce the theme, test general or Biblical knowledge and is a good starter as people drift in during the first ten minutes.

Other ice-breaker ideas include:

- 'What is it?' – well known objects photographed from obscure angles. This may be used to introduce the idea that things are not always what they seem to be.
- 'Silhouettes' of objects/people/places/cartoon characters can introduce the theme 'out of darkness into light'.
- 'Feel Bags' – sealed bags hung around the room, with well known objects inside, can illustrate the theme 'once I was blind ...'

General guidance on using quizzes

Quizzes should be thought about carefully, designed and prepared for the appropriate age group:

- They should not be childish even if they are child-like. Keep your questions at the children's level. Never treat them as being stupid, but keep the quiz and the questions simple enough for all taking part to understand.
- It is important that quizzes should not put people in a situation where they feel threatened.
- Those taking part should always be volunteers and never press-ganged.

- Always think carefully about the questions you are using, so that people are not embarrassed for you or because of you.

- Be considerate in how you deal with those who get an answer wrong. They must not be made to feel 'put down'.

- Quizzes can be either non-competitive or competitive in nature, depending on the need. Sometimes it's good to use the quiz just as a means of setting an atmosphere that is relaxed with no competition between teams.

- However, a competition between teams is good fun, if controlled. There is always the danger of this being hijacked, so ground rules must be clearly spelt out.

- The teams should never be sexist – never boys against girls.

- Always try to have a mixture of ages as well, so that different levels of ability are represented in each team. Arguments are thus done away with.

- Never fix a quiz. The children will always know, and anyway, it's not honest.

- Non-competitive quizzes need careful planning to make sure there is an element of challenge. Cooperative quizzes are where children or adults have to work together to find the answers, by searching around the room, following clues or looking up scripture verses to find the missing words. Another method is to use floor puzzles with one or two making the puzzle and the rest shouting instructions. The team needs to answer a question to gain the next piece of the puzzle (for examples, see page 37).

- Avoid quizzes where one child can lose the whole game for their team, or quizzes that may end up as a draw, for example noughts and crosses.

- Do bear in mind those who have different abilities. You will be working with children and adults, all of whom are different. Some may have disabilities which are visible; in others these may not be so apparent. Not all can read to the same level, or draw well, or even phrase answers well. Some may be physically disabled. Think carefully about the group you are working with, so that everyone, regardless of their abilities, can have a chance to take part. For specific guidance on this, see page 16.

- Never use a quiz just to fill a gap but always as part of the overall programme. Filling a gap will come across as just that, and it would be better not to use one in this way.

Presentation

- It may seem simple to put on a quiz in a service or Mission, but it is not. A good quiz needs careful thought and preparation. Many people give little time to preparing the quiz they will be using, and its impact is lost.

  Effective use of a quiz means working out the best way of presenting it, starting with the visual presentation (see page 10 for resource ideas) through to the questions.

  Poor presentation leaves everyone feeling let down, deflated and with little or no interest in what follows after the quiz. Many quizzes seem to go on for ever, with everyone getting bored. Set your time limit and stick to it. Keep the quiz moving and never let it drag.

- If the audience is restless or rowdy as you prepare to start your quiz, stand still to gain their attention. It will seem like forever! Don't start until you are ready. Breathe slowly, relax your shoulders and then introduce your quiz. Keep calm; don't panic even if you think it's all going wrong.

- Don't raise your voice in an attempt to make yourself heard – it will only add to the noise level. In some situations, a whistle could be used to gain attention but beware of using it too much. Children will soon become used to it and ignore your attempts to gain attention.

- If they become restless during the questions, pause again and wait a few seconds for their attention to return. Allow time for participants to return to their places if appropriate to your quiz.

- Mind your language! Listen to yourself as you give instructions and ask questions. Are you always using the same expressions such as: OK, right, is that clear? Think beforehand of different ways of instructing and questioning a group of people.
- It is important to include as many people as possible in each team. Don't choose the same person each time even if their hand is the only one raised. Encourage others to 'have a go'.
- Questions may be directed at certain age groups. For instance, current chart music questions will probably be answered by the under twenties and rock 'n' roll favourites by the older generation. Adjust your music questions to various age groups.
- In Mission situations or in the open air, it is good to encourage the children to cheer one another on – as a reward for those who have answered the questions, or are taking part in some way. However, in schools or some service situations an alternative is the 'silent cheer' – either thumbs up, or waving hands – the key word is silently!
- When you have decided which option of quiz to use, scoring is a very important part of your presentation.
- There are many ideas to use for scoring systems but simplicity is the watchword. It is important, before you start asking questions, that the children understand how they score for their team; this removes any sense of confusion or cheating.
- You may need to experiment and find out what your particular group enjoys.
- Answering questions may earn points or rewards not only for the team, but also for the person answering. This can encourage many to take part.
- Try to be fair in choosing who answers questions, giving as many people as possible the opportunity to do so.
- Always be prepared: have a dry run, practise your quiz.
- Write out the questions that you will need. Be prepared with extra questions. Always have more than you think you will need.
- Choose someone else to keep the score. This will help eliminate any suspicion of cheating.
- Aim at quizzes that finish after about ten questions – five each side. Finish before the end of the quiz, if necessary, rather than go on too long. It is better to finish a quiz early and leave people wanting more than to bore them.
- Remember to keep your quiz as simple as possible, with clear instructions on how the game works.
- At the end of your activity, try to take time to think through what you have done. How could you have improved your quiz presentation? Make some notes, ask other people what they thought, listen and try to improve.

Using quizzes in programmes

A quiz can be used as part of a programme, written into the running order, introducing a new theme or idea or checking on understanding.

- It could be on-going throughout the programme, like a serial story, linking different aspects of a service. Remember to keep the questions restricted to a certain theme and that the questions run the quiz and not vice versa!
- Alternatively, the quiz may be the main structure of the programme and have the songs, etc linked into it. One way of doing this is to award the next part of the programme as the prize for getting questions correct, for example choosing the next song, and so on. Make sure that the choices are clear and that songs are well known.

- Don't forget to check the duration of the quiz in the overall programme.
- Remember that the type of quiz you are using will affect the atmosphere of the event. Don't put a noisy quiz before a quiet part of the programme as you might not be able to quieten the participants down sufficiently.
- Check with other Mission team members, the service leader or the minister regarding the quiz position and aim in the programme.

Methods of approach

There are many different types of quizzes that you can use in your presentations – some will work for you, others will not. These are listed in full in Section 2 (page 19).

Try them out and find the ones that suit you and your character, as well as the group you are preparing for.

How to make your own quiz

There are many different games that can be made into larger versions or adapted to be used in Missions or churches. It just takes a bit of imagination and effort:

- Always remember to keep them simple in operation and large enough to be seen from the back of the room. Questions need to be prepared beforehand.
- Listen to radio programmes for the types of quizzes they are using. Watch TV shows and see how they present quizzes. This can give you ideas for your own.
- It is possible with the aid of computers to create good quality quizzes of your own.

Here are some different styples of presenting a quiz:

- **Simple quiz** with no equipment or visual aid.
  This takes someone with a large personality, who is comfortable with presenting things to groups of people, can think on their feet and doesn't get flustered easily. It may involve making up questions on the spot, but this is best avoided, if at all possible. Questions can be directed at various age groups, for example: under tens, between ten and twenty and so on. Remember older members of the congregation may be reticent to take part. This presentation relies totally on the personality of the quiz leader.
- **Board games** are known to all of us, from Snakes and Ladders through to Monopoly. With a little imagination and practise, some board games can make excellent quizzes.
- **Music or video-based**. Snippets of favourite programmes, theme tunes or songs from the charts can be pre-recorded, leaving teams to guess the titles or performers.
- **Participation quizzes** are where those attending the activity become part of the actual quiz, eg human noughts and crosses (see page 19).
- **Objects**, seen or unseen can also be the basis of a quiz. The teams are given a series of clues relating to each object – they guess what the object is and who it may refer to in the Bible.

For example, a bag of coins with the following clues will relate to Matthew the tax collector:
- I collected taxes.
- I followed Jesus.
- There is a New Testament book with the same name as mine.

Equipment and resources

It is important that those at the back of the audience can see what is going on as well as hear clearly. Therefore, quizzes are made clearer by the use of a large display board, such as one of those listed below:

- **Metal boards** – These sit on easels and use strips of self-adhesive magnetic tape to secure the quiz sheet on to the board. Any counters used can also be securely positioned on the board.
- **Velcro boards** – These are made of looped nylon stretched over a sheet of board, preferably of approximately 6 mm thickness. The game and counters are attached to this by hook nylon pads which are stuck to the back of them. Any counters are easily moved using this system.
- **White boards** – These are great for non-permanent quizzes, such as noughts and crosses, or 'guess the drawing' types of quiz. They are easily cleaned off and portable.

If you are presenting a quiz that uses some form of visual focus, ie a board game, then this should be displayed in a format large enough for everyone to see. Try standing at the back of a crowd to determine the size of equipment required for everyone to see it easily. I would suggest that a quiz presented on 122cm x 91cm sheets of card is big enough for most Missions, groups or church activities.

Materials to create your own quizzes

Any of the high street art shops or local craft suppliers should be able to supply adhesive strips, Velcro pads, gummed paper and craft pens for colouring large quiz boards.

You can purchase acetate sheets (both clear and coloured sheets) from most office suppliers and equipment like skittles, etc can be bought from most major toy stores.

Materials to create your own boards

- Magnetic, Velcro, white boards or plastic boards, may be purchased by researching online websites or your local DIY store.
- Your local 'scrap store' is a valuable resource for all sorts of materials you can use to create quizzes with.
- Badges may be bought ready-made or the equipment can be obtained to make your own. The company listed below also produces stickers, patches and much more. For more details contact:
  Enterprise Products
  Unit 18a
  Station Road Business Park
  Barnack
  Stamford
  Lincs
  PE9 3DW

Overhead projectors

More churches are using overhead projectors in their services and children's activities, and these can be used effectively for quizzes. Projectors need to be carefully set up and focused before the meeting begins. They have the advantage of showing a large visual on a screen or a wall. The acetate sheets are also easy to store.

- Again, ensure that any writing on the acetate is visible from the back of the room.
- Board quizzes can be photocopied on to acetate sheets and used over and over again.
- Counters for quizzes on overhead projectors need careful thought, as anything solid will not show as a colour but as a black solid on the screen. Either use different shaped card, or use coloured acetate shapes.
- An overhead projector can also be used to enlarge the quizzes in this book on to sheets of card. Photocopy the quiz on to an acetate sheet. Use the projector to enlarge the picture on to your sheet of card, focus it and then draw around the image. Colour it in and even if you have few artistic skills, the quiz will look good.

Using a computer

If you are proficient at using a package such as PowerPoint and your church has the facilities to project onto a screen using a computer and projector then this would be another method of showing your quizzes to great advantage.

Dice and spinner

You may wish to make large dice or a spinner to allow all team members to see clearly what number has been thrown. Enlarge and cut out the templates on the following page:

Push a pencil or a piece of dowelling through the middle of the hexagonal template to make it spin.

Make this into a die – either with numbers on each square or dots.

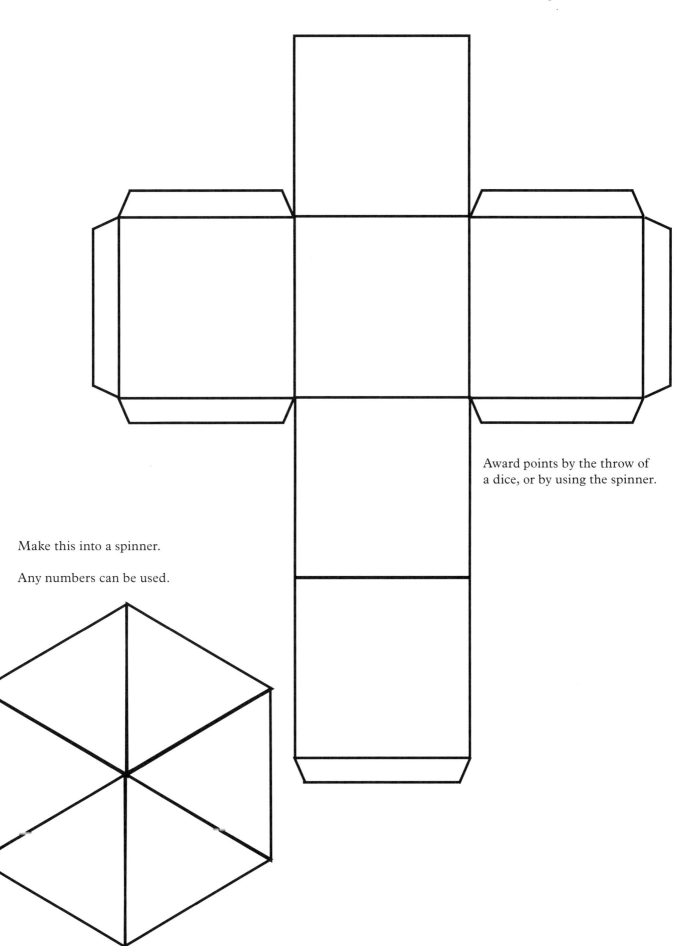

Award points by the throw of
a dice, or by using the spinner.

Make this into a spinner.

Any numbers can be used.

How to create questions for quizzes

You may feel confident enough to write your own quiz questions. Alternatively, you may wish to use the quiz questions set out in Section 3 (page 82). Either way, it is important that the questions used for your quiz reflect the purpose of the quiz, either as revision or to introduce a new subject:

- Plan your questions carefully, making sure that they are easy to understand. Think carefully about whether there may be two correct answers to your question.

- When working in an environment where there may be children or adults with little or no knowledge of Scripture, it is important to encourage them with questions that may refer to the local church or the local community eg 'Who is the vicar?'. In a Mission situation, try using questions relating to team members, eg 'Who drives a green Mini?' You could also use questions related to sport or general knowledge. From this base, you can start to build questions relating to your subject.

Questions for quizzes generally fall into one of two categories:

- **Factual questions** – which ask: Who? When? Where?

  These types of questions enable the teachers or leaders to check that the details of a passage from the Bible have been retained.

  So, for example, the question: 'Who provided the fish that swallowed Jonah?' is better than the question: 'Did God provide the fish that swallowed Jonah?' The first question asks the child to think through part of the story, whereas the second requires only a yes or no answer.

- **Interpretative questions** – which ask: How? Why? What?

  These are used to check a child understands the teaching aspects of the story. Have they understood what you have been teaching (not just the facts of the story, but your application)?

  So, you could phrase your question in the following manner: 'Why did God provide the fish to swallow Jonah?' The child then has to think through the reasons for God's actions.

- Therefore when planning your questions always bear in mind the words: Who? When? Where? How? Why? What? These can often be the best way of revising the teaching through quiz questions.

- You can alter the way you ask questions. You may wish to use any combination of the following types of question – by mixing the various ways of asking a question – or you may wish to use the same style throughout the quiz.

Try some of these:

- True or false.

- Multiple choice – you can experiment with the whole team choosing an answer to the question ie hands up for answer A, B or C. The majority decision is taken as the answer.

- Who am I? with clues gradually given to the identity of the person or object.

- Spot the mistake.

- Jumbled names or places or books of the Bible.

- Matching pairs.

- Fill in the missing word.

- Questions that bring out the meaning of the story. (See Section 3, page xx, for specific examples.)

Remember when planning your quiz that children will fall into two types: those who are confident and willing to take part and those who are nervous or reticent in answering questions. It is suggested that you keep your questions simple enough for 80% of the children to understand. Remember, as well, that up to 20% will never take part.

Dealing with wrong answers is always difficult. Try to respond in a positive way to a wrong answer, perhaps with statements like, 'That's not quite the right answer,' or, 'That's not what I'm looking for.'

When you have the right answer, explain why the other answer was wrong. Try to commend the children who give the wrong answers. Never poke fun at them, but encourage them.

Quizzes for different age groups

You will need to have some understanding of children's development so that, when working with them, it is possible to produce quizzes and questions that are aimed at the right age group, making the most of their abilities.

The following details are given only as a general guide to understanding child development and therefore may not match up exactly to a particular child.

The under 8s

What are they like?

Believe what they are told and talk naturally about God. They think literally.

Have a short attention span – are full of energy and very active.

Have a limited vocabulary.

Older children love to help adults.

Learn by using their senses: sight, smell, hearing, touch, and taste.

Find it difficult to make the distinction between fact and fantasy.

Enjoy and learn through repetition.

They often have fears and concerns. They need lots of encouragement and praise. They like to be noticed.

What to bear in mind when planning your quiz

Be careful about using picture language; the child may take you literally. Make instructions for quizzes and games clear.

Do not expect them to stick at one activity for very long. Have lots of variety in your programme. Use quizzes with lots of actions. Keep it short.

They understand more words than they use, so word your questions carefully. Plan ahead.

Give them every opportunity to help you, even in presenting the quiz. Include quizzes and questions that use the senses.

Try not to mix fact and fantasy together. Encourage the use of the imagination by, 'What do you think they were feeling?' type of questions.

Use familiar language and questions that repeat the story or teaching, to check they have understood.

Get to know them as individuals, listen to them and respond whenever possible with praise and encouragement. Try to speak and act towards them in a manner worth imitating.

8 to 11s

What are they like?	What to bear in mind when planning your quiz
They are physically energetic, and enjoy gaining more manipulative skills.	Plenty of change in activity. Not too much sitting still. Quizzes need to be fast and sharp.
Enjoy the latest craze, but these are short-lived.	Do not pursue your quiz to the point of boredom; quit while they still want more. Be an enthusiast, but do not pretend.
They are eager to learn new things.	Try to make sure that you are not repeating the same thing over and over again. Try presenting new quizzes, basing them on things they already have an interest in: such as computer games, football or horses.
They continue to think literally: dealing only in the concrete rather than in the abstract.	Avoid figurative language, and abstract ideas. Look at the wording of your questions. Does it have a double meaning?
Vocabulary is still limited.	Keep the questions and your vocabulary simple and short.
With the start of puberty, earlier in girls than boys, they start to become self-conscious.	Try to prevent the self-conscious child being exposed to ridicule. Avoid drawing attention to those who are different in the group. Don't talk down to them.
Increasingly independent.	Allow them to take part, and perhaps to present the quiz, even if it is slower.
Strong sense of justice – cries of, 'That's not fair!' Starting to develop a moral sense of right and wrong. Still influenced by adults. They see things in black and white terms.	Explain the reasons for the rules of the quiz and your actions. They appreciate knowing why.

11 plus age group

What are they like?	What to bear in mind when planning your quiz
Self-critical and self-conscious. Also very sensitive to criticism from others.	Be careful how you handle wrong answers. Give them positive encouragement.
Start of the growth spurt. Become conscious of being clumsy, and of their size or figure.	Avoid making fun of them. Be sensitive to their feelings: recognise that some may not be good at coping with taking part in games and quizzes.
Starting to mature physically. Sexually curious.	Try not to be shocked or embarrassed by things they say, or the comments they make. Ignore silly answers.
Strong sense of justice.	Avoid choosing your favourite in the group. Make sure rules and scoring are fair. Have mixed teams if possible.
More sophisticated in their ways of learning. Things are quickly labelled, 'boring'. Still have a fairly short attention span, and react negatively to anything that seems like school.	Try to be imaginative and resourceful in providing different ways of reinforcing their learning. Try to use quizzes that involve working together.
Starting to question assumptions and attitudes.	Avoid jargon and clichés. Don't talk down to them.
Membership of a particular group or gang is very important. Desperate need to be accepted.	Try to include as many as possible in your activity. Be aware of the quieter group members. Find ways that will build and encourage.

Adults

Adults and older teens will experience similar problems of embarrassment, learning difficulties and awkwardness. Use the guidelines to deal sympathetically with them. They need to be accepted as part of the whole activity and not just as spectators.

Quizzes for different abilities

The Problem

Many church and young people's groups have members who have different abilities. Differences may be caused by hearing problems, physical, emotional or mental disabilities or even limited learning ability.

Not only are the causes varied but, even within the different groups, the degree of disability is varied. For some, language skills may be a problem; for others, concentration is poor; whilst for others it may be difficult to grasp concepts. Therefore, there is no one way of coping with children who have varying degrees of learning difficulties.

The Warnock Report (1977)[*] gave some indication of the extent of the problem. 1.8% of the school population were in special schools and 6.5% of the school population were in special classes within their schools. If this is added to the figure for those children within the class for whom special arrangements are made, this figure represents about 20% of children with some sort of learning difficulty.

Meeting the Problem

A differently-abled child may manifest some of the following problems:

- be unable to understand the spoken word,
- be unable to put thoughts into words,
- be unable to follow any logical argument,
- have difficulty in concentrating,
- have difficulty in reading, unable to read at all,
- be unable to generalise,
- have difficulty in remembering.

These may be covered up by disruptive behaviour. Children who have been damaged emotionally may appear to have the same problems but this may be due to a different root cause.

What help is available for you?

There is very little specific material available if you have differently-abled children in your groups. However, there are some general guidelines for preparing quizzes as well as general programmes.

When preparing your quiz bear in mind the following:

- How are you expecting children to participate in your quiz? Might it present problems to a child with learning difficulties, etc?
- Try not to humiliate them.
- Bible reading out loud can be embarrassing.
- Any reading may be difficult for some.
- Memory work may be impossible.
- Worksheets – check size of print, layout, reading ability needed.
- Quizzes need to reflect the needs of all taking part. For example, if the quiz involves running around, will all the children be able to take part? What about the child in the wheelchair, or with a broken leg or arm? Do you need to arrange a one-to-one helper?

[*] The Scope of Special Education Parliamentary Paper, Department of Education and Science (ISBN 0 10172 120 X).

Needs of children with learning difficulties

They need:

- Frequent success – keep questions and activities at their level.
- To be thought well of – don't laugh at them but with them, even when they make a mistake.
- To be valued whatever they do – never try to judge an individual's behaviour.
- To be liked and accepted. To take part; to express themselves without ridicule – be patient if they can't form their answer quickly.
- To have the chance to contribute, create and to influence – make sure they get their turn. Don't ignore them or their contribution, but try to avoid making them the centre of attention.

Key principles:

These may also relate to more able children and adults.

- There is a need for constant feedback to confirm that the message and teaching has been understood. Quizzes are an ideal way to do this in a fun environment.
- Make the most of informal conversation.
- Work mainly in small groups of six children, if possible. Each group has its own quiz.
- Personal relationship between worker and child is crucial to develop.
- Identify what the child can do – and praise that.
- Aim to make one major point.
- Use a variety of presentation ideas.
- Repetition is the key to learning.
- Keep each item in your programme short and to the point.
- Link teaching to knowledge and experiences.

Positive aims:

- Present teaching and activities to as many senses as possible.
- Work on team/group projects.
- Expect constructive positive attitudes from them.
- Use a simple Bible translation.
- Give attention to children in their group equally, regardless of abilities.
- Use lower case lettering wherever possible. Words printed in capitals are harder to read.

In summary, it is important before selecting your quiz and questions that you think through these issues.

Try the following questions as a quick checklist:

- What are the needs of my group?
- Have I accounted for each child's needs in the group?
- Is there anyone who will struggle with this quiz?

We hope that you will now try out the quizzes and questions in the rest of this book.

And finally...

Remember the quizzes in this book are photocopiable and can be enlarged to A3 or A2 size.

We have tried to give some guidance in your use of quizzes and questions by suggesting various age groups. However, these are not rigid instructions and you may find them suitable for other ages or situations.

Unless otherwise stated all the questions are based on the Bible text of the New International Version.

The questions have been arranged in various categories but feel free to pick and choose from each section. Or better still, have a go at writing your own.

Prepare yourself and your quiz carefully and thoroughly. Speak clearly but, most important of all ... HAVE FUN!

1 Human noughts & crosses

USES

It is possible to use this as an ongoing quiz for a series of events, such as a Mission, or as a one-off quiz in a service or special event. It is suitable for all ages.

EQUIPMENT NEEDED

- Three rows of three chairs, arranged in a similar way to the grid used in normal noughts and crosses,

- nine pieces of card, marked with a cross on one side and a nought on the other, suitable quiz questions.

HOW TO PLAY

Divide your group into two teams: noughts and crosses.

The game is played like normal noughts and crosses, each team answering a question alternately. The child that answers the question correctly for their team chooses where they would like to sit, holding the card with their team's identification showing – nought or cross. Whenever three human noughts or crosses find themselves in a row, they win that round for their team.

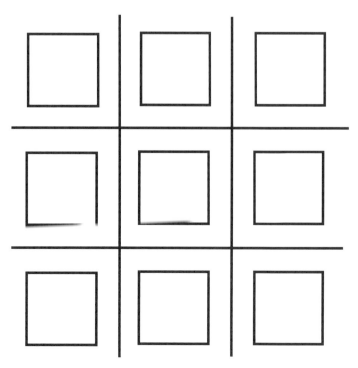

2 Music or film quiz

USES

When using music or film clips make sure that they are suitable for the age group you are using them with, and that you do not infringe copyright.

Remember that anyone with a visual or hearing disability may find it difficult to join in.

EQUIPMENT NEEDED

With the availability of DVD players, video recorders and portable music systems it is possible to incorporate audio and visual material as part of a quiz. Pre-record some short snippets from either chart music or well known films or dramas. It would be good to have a selection of both Christian and non-Christian material.

HOW TO PLAY

Make sure that the music or film clip will be known by the group. Explain your points scoring system, which may be one point for each correct answer. Tell them what answer you will be expecting: the name of the film, or the actor in the clip, the musician or group they are in, the film or song title.

Divide your group into one of the following to take part in the quiz:

- two teams competing against each other,
- small groups competing for points for their overall team,
- pairs competing against each other,
- family groups (Remember to include those who have no family with them.),
- different interest groups competing against each other. For example, football, cricket, show jumping, etc.

Play the piece of music or film clip. The teams then write their answers down, keeping it secret from the other teams. When you have played through all your music or film questions, read out the answers, or collect the answers in. Award points to find the winning team.

With younger children it is best to divide the group into two teams and to play the film or music clip to the teams alternately. Give the teams time to answer before moving on to the next clip. Award points for correct answers. Appoint a group leader to record their answers.

3 Misfits quiz

USES

A simple to produce quiz that is suitable for most age groups.

EQUIPMENT NEEDED

- Pictures from magazines. Choose those that your group will be familiar with. These should be mounted on to card and need to be full page in size, usually A4;
- a board to display them on,
- questions for each side, at least five per side,
- a whistle.

When you have mounted the pictures on to card, divide the picture into three sections. Cut them up so that each section can be mixed up with the rest of the pictures you are going to use. Put them around the edge of the board.

HOW TO PLAY

Make sure that it is clear which picture pieces are for which team to try and match together, otherwise a 'free for all' will take place. If space is at a premium, you may wish to place each team's pieces in a container for them to take out when they try to make the pictures up. It is best to have no more than five pictures for each side.

Ask your questions alternately by team. As you are given correct answers, that child comes to the front. When you have asked all the questions, you should have five members of each team standing on either side of the board. The task for them is to match up as many of the pictures that they can in the time allowed them.

It is usually best to have one question for leaders from each side, so the children have an adult to assist them in the matching of pieces.

At the end of one minute, blow your whistle to signal the end of their time. The team with the most matching pieces wins. You could award points for each correct piece matched, say five points per piece of picture correctly matched.

4 Quicksand

USES

This quiz can be used with those who have reading ability, and also have some knowledge of using the Bible. Scripture verses need to be looked up as part of the quiz. Try to use a modern version, if possible.

The game is about faithfulness and unfaithfulness (or unreliability) and is probably best understood by children of seven and over.

EQUIPMENT NEEDED

- Dice or spinner,
- a counter for each team,
- a copy of the quiz big enough for them to see, or enough copies for the number of groups you have,
- suitable quiz questions.

HOW TO PLAY

Divide your group of children into either two teams, or into small groups to play, then divide each small group into two teams.

Each team answers questions alternately, and when they give a correct answer they get the chance to move their team's counter across the quicksand.

The boulders show a possible way across this stretch of quicksand.

Using a dice or spinner, see who can reach the path on the other side first. Look out, though – some boulders are more reliable as footholds than others. If you land on one with a reference, look it up. If it is about faithfulness, move on two extra steps. If it is about unfaithfulness or unreliability, retreat quickly by two steps. You must follow the boulders in numerical sequence. The first team to cross the quicksand, safely, wins.

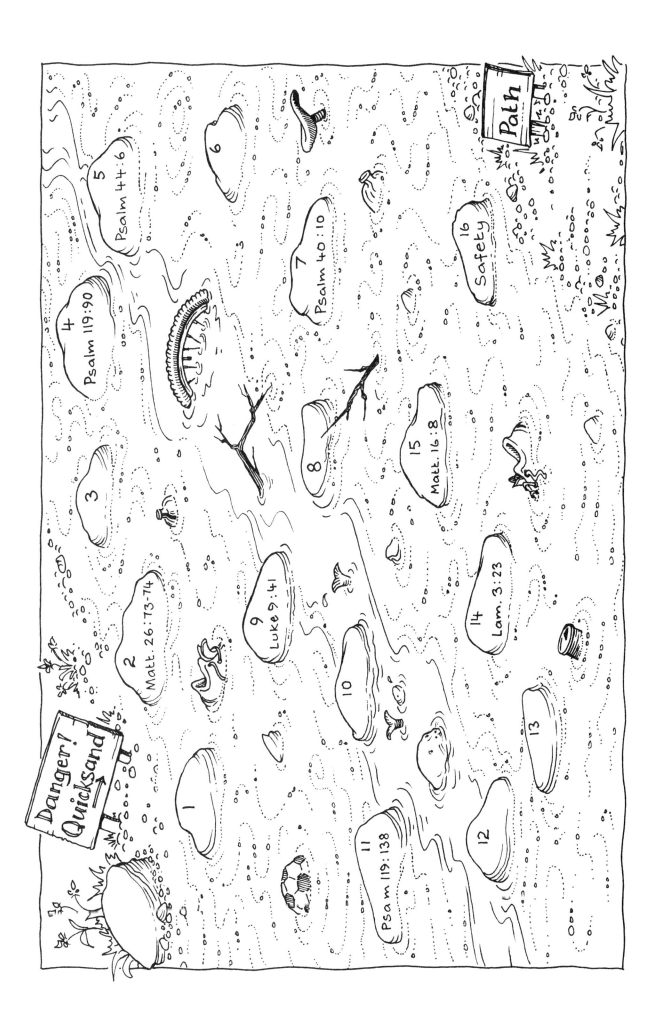

23

5 The forfeits game

USES

This quiz is best used in small groups, either in Junior Church situations, or as part of a group activity during Holiday clubs.

It is probably best suited to use with the 7 plus age group, due to the forfeits that are part of the quiz.

EQUIPMENT NEEDED

- Dice or a spinner,
- individual markers or counters,
- a copy of the game large enough for your group to see easily.

HOW TO PLAY

The game is played in your group. You may wish to have a special number to start your travel along the course. The first person to the home square wins the game. However, forfeits must be carried out if at all possible.

THE FORFEITS GAME

HOME

Tidy up the room when the game is over.

Give up your next go to someone else.

Extra Throw

Offer to help with the shopping.

Tell someone what is their best quality.

Volunteer to do an extra job at home.

Extra Throw

Say something nice about another person's clothes.

START

THE FORFEIT GAME MOTTO
Do not forget to do good and to help one another, because these are the sacrifices that please God.
Hebrews 13:16 (GNB).

6 Game of David's life

USES

These two quizzes are specifically about David's life, and are good for recapping about his life following a teaching programme within your church or Holiday club.

They are best used with small groups.

Choose the quiz which relates best to your age group.

EQUIPMENT NEEDED

- Dice or a spinner,
- Individual markers or counters,
- a copy of the game large enough for your group to see easily.

HOW TO PLAY

The game is played in your group. You may wish to have a special number to start your travel along the course. The first person to the home square wins the game.

Game of David's life

Solomon will be the next king.

David gives a lot of money to build God a temple. Move on 1 place.

David is kind to Barzillai. Move on 1 place.

Absalom is killed. Missed a turn.

Absalom goes to war against David. Go back 2 places.

David's son Absalom wants to be king. Miss a turn.

Nathan speaks to David and he repents. Move on 1 place.

David steals Bathsheba. Miss a turn.

Saul dies and David becomes king. Move 2 places.

David is sad because Jonathan and Saul are dead. Miss a turn.

David fights the Philistines again and wins. Move on place.

The Covenant Box arrives in Jerusalem. Move on 1 place.

David is kind to Jonathan's son, Mephibosheth. Move on 1 place.

David spares Saul's life. Move on 1 place.

David hides in a cave. Miss a turn.

David has to flee from the palace. Go back 3 places.

David fights the Philistines at Keilah and wins. Move 1 place.

Jonathan saves David. Move on 1 place.

Saul tries to kill David. Miss a turn.

David wins many victories for Saul. Move 3 places.

David is annointed by Samuel. Move two places

David plays harp for King Saul.

Goliath challenges Israelites. Go back one place.

David tries on Saul's armour. Miss a turn.

David fights Goliath and kills him. Move on 1 place.

Jonathan and David make friends. Move on 1 place.

David marries Saul's daughter. Move on 1 place.

Saul becomes jealous of David. Miss a turn.

I'm sorry God

7 Running away

USES

A game based on the story of Jonah. It is ideal for services or Holiday clubs where Jonah's story has been the basis of teaching.

This quiz is ideal for use with small groups aged 5 and upwards.

EQUIPMENT NEEDED

- Dice or a spinner,
- individual markers or counters,
- a copy of the game large enough for your group to see easily.

The game is played in your group. You may wish to have a special number to start your travel along the course. The first person to the home square wins the game.

Running away

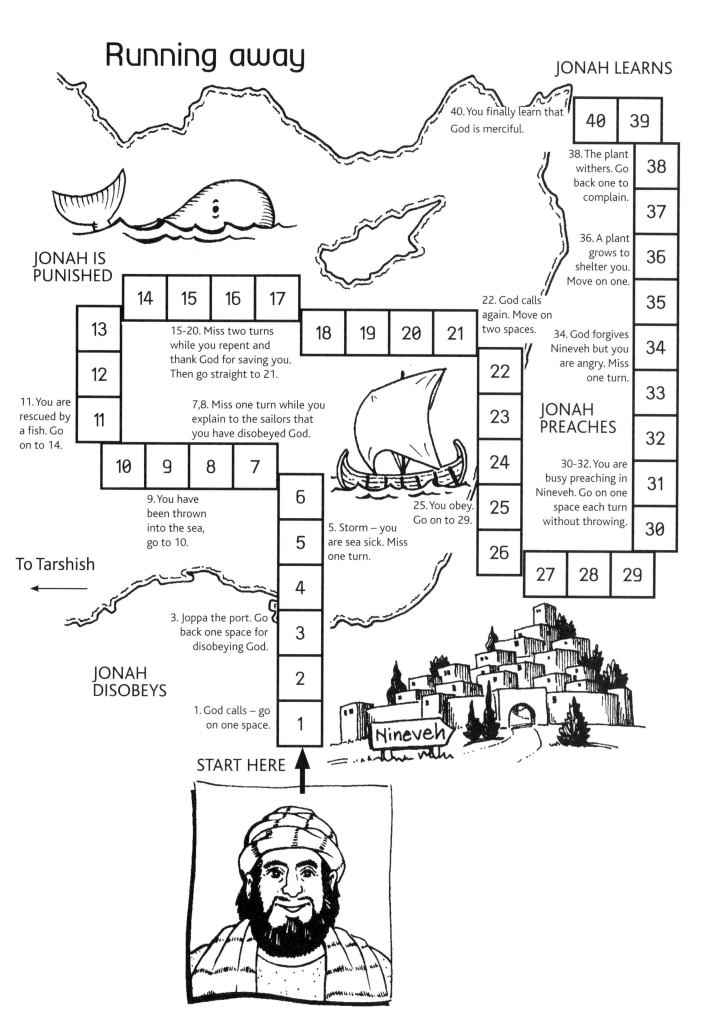

JONAH LEARNS

40. You finally learn that God is merciful.

| 40 | 39 |

38. The plant withers. Go back one to complain.

| 38 |
| 37 |

36. A plant grows to shelter you. Move on one.

| 36 |
| 35 |

22. God calls again. Move on two spaces.

34. God forgives Nineveh but you are angry. Miss one turn.

| 34 |
| 33 |

JONAH PREACHES

30-32. You are busy preaching in Nineveh. Go on one space each turn without throwing.

| 32 |
| 31 |
| 30 |

| 27 | 28 | 29 |

JONAH IS PUNISHED

| 14 | 15 | 16 | 17 |

| 13 |
| 12 |
| 11 |

15-20. Miss two turns while you repent and thank God for saving you. Then go straight to 21.

| 18 | 19 | 20 | 21 |

| 22 |
| 23 |
| 24 |
| 25 |
| 26 |

7,8. Miss one turn while you explain to the sailors that you have disobeyed God.

11. You are rescued by a fish. Go on to 14.

| 10 | 9 | 8 | 7 |

9. You have been thrown into the sea, go to 10.

25. You obey. Go on to 29.

| 6 |
| 5 |
| 4 |
| 3 |
| 2 |
| 1 |

5. Storm – you are sea sick. Miss one turn.

To Tarshish

3. Joppa the port. Go back one space for disobeying God.

JONAH DISOBEYS

1. God calls – go on one space.

START HERE

Nineveh

8 Abraham's journey

This quiz traces the journey of Abraham from Ur to Canaan. It revises any teaching on Abraham and is best played in small groups. This quiz is for anyone aged 5 and upwards.

- Dice or a spinner,
- individual markers or counters,
- a copy of the game large enough for your group to see easily.

The game is played in your group. You may wish to have a special number to start your travel along the course. The first person to the home square wins the game.

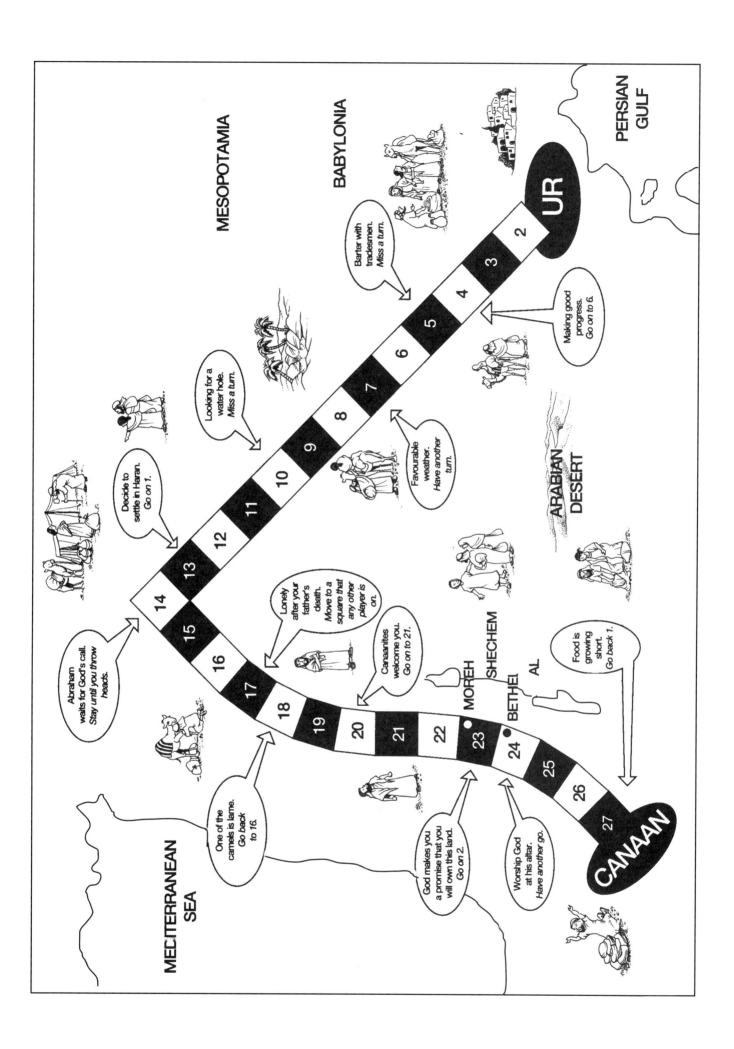

31

9 Quiz rings

USES

This quiz can be used in all types of situations. It is good for breaking down tension and barriers.

There is no real age limit to this one, but care should be exercised with the under 7s.

EQUIPMENT NEEDED

- A ball of string,
- a pair of round-ended scissors,
- two plastic containers,
- a collection of curtain rings (The number will depend on the answers to your questions.),
- your questions – carefully worked out.

HOW TO PLAY

Divide the participants into two teams and ask each team to line up and then sit down.

Each team threads a length of string through the hands of all the team members.

One person from each team holds the rings at the back of the team while another, at the front end of the team, has a container into which the rings will eventually be counted.

The quiz leader asks both teams at the same time a question that has a number for an answer.

For example: How many spies went into Canaan? [Answer: 12.]

When each team has the answer they tell their ring holder, who then counts out the required number of rings (in this case 12) and threads them on to the string. Then all the rings are passed – one by one – from one team member to the next until they reach the front. When all the rings are at the front, the person holding the container stands up, and counts the rings into their container.

Points are only awarded to the team that comes first. Five points are awarded each time a team wins.

Ask ten questions in total, then add up the score for the winning team to be announced.

10 Tin can targets

USES

This quiz is suitable for all ages to take part in, including the under 5s.

A quiz of this type can be used in many situations, especially Missions, Holiday clubs and some family services.

EQUIPMENT NEEDED

- 10 empty tin cans (baked beans tins are ideal) washed and cleaned, and numbered clearly 1 to 10. The number will be the score for the can you have knocked down. Pile these into a pyramid,
- something safe and soft to throw at the cans – bean bags are ideal,
- suitable quiz questions.

HOW TO PLAY

Set up a 'shooting' range. Mark a base line to stand on, with the tins about 2–3 metres away on a table. Adjust this distance to suit the group you are working with.

Divide the group into two teams. Ask your questions alternately. Whoever answers correctly from the teams, tries to knock down as many cans as possible. The score is obtained by adding the numbers on the cans that are not standing up. Each person has two shots.

At the end of the quiz the highest score wins. Announce the winning team.

11 Wak a rat

USES

This quiz idea is best suited to Holiday clubs or mid-week meetings. As it involves some dexterity, it works best with young people of 11 years and upwards.

EQUIPMENT NEEDED

- A plastic or foam baseball bat,
- a rat (not a real one!) made from material stuffed with pebbles to give it weight,
- a short length of plastic drainpipe,
- a length of floorboard,
- a step ladder,
- suitable quiz questions.

Follow the instructions opposite to make this quiz presentation idea.

HOW TO PLAY

Two teams answer questions alternately. The team member who answers the question correctly tries to hit the rat as it comes out of the pipe. The rat is dropped down the tube by the quiz leader or an assistant.

Hitting the rat scores points in the following way:

If the rat is hit while passing the 25, 20 or 10 zone, then these points are scored for the team.

Extra points can be awarded, if desired, by hitting the rat on the body only. You may wish to award an extra 5 points.

The rat does tend to fall quickly. Therefore it is suggested that, for younger children, the rat's tail should be made longer, so that it can be lowered into the tube allowing it to sit as far down as possible. When it is released it does not fall as fast and smaller children have a chance to hit it.

15cm body
filled with
pebbles

String tail
60 cm long

Fixed to step ladder, the
Wak a rat pipe and score
board works well

183 cm

92 cm

1.15 cm

25

20

10

Drain pipe

Fix drain
pipe to
board with
screws.

Floor Board

12 Balloon burst

USES

A great quiz for all types of meetings, but care should be taken with the under 5s, as bursting balloons can scare them.

EQUIPMENT NEEDED

- A selection (ten or more) of large brightly-coloured balloons,
- slips of paper,
- a pin for bursting the balloons (Keep it somewhere safe!),
- suitable quiz questions.

HOW TO PLAY

Write scores from 10 to 100 on the slips of paper. It is suggested that ten slips would be enough, numbered 10, 20, 30, etc. Roll these up and place one inside each of the ten balloons. Then blow up the balloons.

Divide your participants into two teams. Ask questions alternately. Whoever answers the question chooses and bursts a balloon. The score is on the slip of paper inside the balloon. At the end of the quiz, add up the score and announce the winning team.

To make things a bit more exciting, add a bonus prize inside two balloons. These could be either double all your team's points, or win a prize for that person.

You could fill the balloons with confetti to make things even more fun, but do remember to clean up behind you so that it is not left for the cleaners to do.

Always pick up the pieces of burst balloons, so that small children will not pick them up and possibly swallow them.

13 Floor or board puzzle

USES

Floor puzzles are great in situations where you have a lot of space, such as Missions or Holiday clubs, but are generally not suitable for church services.

These are great for just about all ages, as long as you ensure that the picture and the size of the puzzle pieces are suitable for younger children.

EQUIPMENT NEEDED

- Two copies of the same picture (commercially available posters are ideal),
- two large sheets of card,
- suitable quiz questions.

Stick the pictures to the card, and cut them into five pieces. Spread these around the perimeter of your venue. If you are putting the puzzle on to boards, ensure enough magnetic tape or Velcro is used to hold the pieces to the display board.

HOW TO PLAY

Two teams compete for their pieces to the puzzle. Before they do this, they must answer five questions correctly. Ask questions of each team alternately. The person who answers correctly is chosen and comes to the front. They must wait until five people from each team are chosen. This group then have to rush around the room collecting the pieces of the puzzle and putting it together correctly. The first team to do so wins.

14 String quiz

USES

This quiz can be used with most age groups, but it works best with 5–11s.
   This is a great quiz for Holiday clubs and family services.

EQUIPMENT NEEDED

- A ball of string,
- container with a lid (an ice cream tub is ideal),
- suitable quiz questions.

Cut ten pieces of string into various lengths and put them into your container with one end of each piece hanging out.

HOW TO PLAY

Divide your children into two teams. Choose a 'knot person' from each of the two teams. It is their job to tie the pieces of string together with knots. Check that each knot person can actually tie knots! Ask them to stand at the front next to the quiz leader.
   Ask questions of each team alternately. The person answering correctly comes and chooses a piece of string. As the team answers more questions correctly, these pieces of string are tied together by the knot person. The team, at the end of the quiz, with the longest length of knotted string wins.

15 Suitcase

USES

This is a quiz that goes down well in almost any situation or service. A fun quiz suitable for any age group.

EQUIPMENT NEEDED

- A selection of suitcases (boxes could be used) of varying sizes.
- A series of numbers such as 5, 8, 103, etc. written on individual sheets of paper, one placed inside each suitcase. It is suggested that the score has no relation to the size of the suitcase used, or the older children will work out the suitcase with the highest score.
- Suitable quiz questions.

HOW TO PLAY

Divide the group into two teams. Have a pile of suitcases at the front (ten is a good number). When a child answers a question correctly that child then comes to the front and chooses a suitcase. They then open it to find out the score they have won for their team. When all the cases have been opened, or time has run out, add up the scores to find the winner.

16 Skittles

USES

This quiz game requires plenty of room and works well even with the very youngest of children.

EQUIPMENT NEEDED

- Ten skittles or the equivalent; perhaps plastic washing-up bottles or squash bottles, half-filled with sand,
- a large ball to roll at them,
- suitable quiz questions.

HOW TO PLAY

Set up your skittle alley. This needs to be about 2 metres in length for the younger children, but can be up to 4 metres for older children.

Appoint a score keeper.

The aim is to answer a question for your team, by raising your hand. A correct answer gains your team 10 points. The same child can then roll the ball at the skittles. The team scores by the number of skittles that each person knocks down. Therefore, the maximum score is 10. Add this to the 10 points for answering the question.

Set the skittles up again after each question.

At the end of the game announce the winning team.

17 Boxes

USES

This is a quiz used mainly in Holiday clubs and Beach Missions, but can be used in many different situations.

It is especially good for those between the ages of 5 and 7.

EQUIPMENT NEEDED

- A collection of different-sized boxes,
- suitable quiz questions.

HOW TO PLAY

Ask each team a question in turn. The child that answers correctly then chooses a box. The idea is to see which team has built the tallest pile by the end of the questions.

If a team's pile of boxes topples over before the end of the quiz, then they have to start again.

ULTIMATE
Quizzes

18 Pairs

USES

This quiz works well in most situations and has been used on Beach Missions, Holiday clubs, mid-week clubs and family services.

It is suitable for children aged 5 years old and upwards.

EQUIPMENT NEEDED

- A collection of pairs (see examples from matching pairs on page 83), each pair is written on to card, making two cards for each pair. Make a total of 16 cards in all. Write the numbers 1 to 16 on the opposite side of the card, for identification;
- a board to display them on, or an overhead projector,
- a selection of questions to ask each team. These can be either about the pairs you are using, or about specific teaching that you wish to revise.

HOW TO PLAY

The 16 numbered cards are displayed on the board. Each team takes it in turns to try and find a pair, by answering questions alternately. The team who finds the most pairs wins. You will need to remove each pair as they are matched up. The person who answers correctly chooses a pair of cards. If there is a match, award 10 points. No match, no points.

There are no points for the last pair on the board.

It is useful if the pairs can be arranged to give humorous answers. For example, Bible pairs:

- Balaam and his donkey,
- Daniel and the lions.

It is helpful for those with little Bible knowledge to have some other pairings:

- Pooh and Piglet,
- Postman Pat and Jess,
- Thomas the Tank Engine and the Fat Controller.

19 Sticky ball

USES

A quiz that is good for even the very youngest of children, useful in a club or mid-week meeting.

EQUIPMENT NEEDED

- A board covered in hook nylon material, this needs to be marked out like the illustration below,
- four balls covered in hoop nylon, so that the balls will stick to the board (these can be bought in most of the larger toy shops),
- a series of questions.

HOW TO PLAY

Divide your group into two teams and ask questions alternately. When a question is answered correctly by a team member, that team member comes out and has two attempts at throwing the ball at the board target. Wherever the ball sticks, gives the score. If the ball doesn't stick, there is no score. When all the questions have been asked, add up the score to see which team has won.

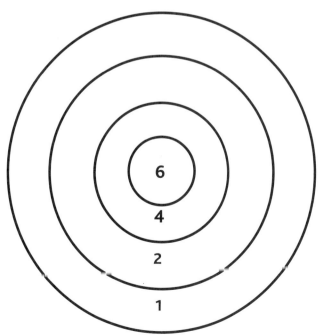

20 Dominoes

This quiz is great for all the family as no Bible knowledge is needed – all the information is contained on the dominoes. It is a good teaching game that can be used for just about any service or event.

It is suitable for even the youngest of children, but great fun for all ages.

- Dominoes large enough for the venue you are using:
- For example, in a Mission venue each domino could be 25 cm x 12 cm,
- a board to display them on, suitable quiz questions (see illustration below).

When making the dominoes they need to be colour-coded, so you know when you have a match. For example (see illustration above), the number '4' could be coloured red, and so could 'Gospels'.

Divide the group into two teams.

Place any one domino on the board, then ask questions alternately by team. The question should relate to the domino on the board.

For example: How many Gospels are there? [Answer: four.]

How many loaves did Jesus use to feed the five thousand? [Answer: five.]

If the question is answered correctly, the next domino in sequence is added to the board, until all the dominoes are used. The blank domino guarantees a choice right at the end of the game. The winner is the team that puts down the last domino.

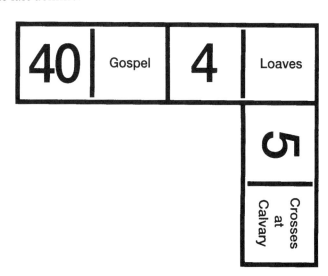

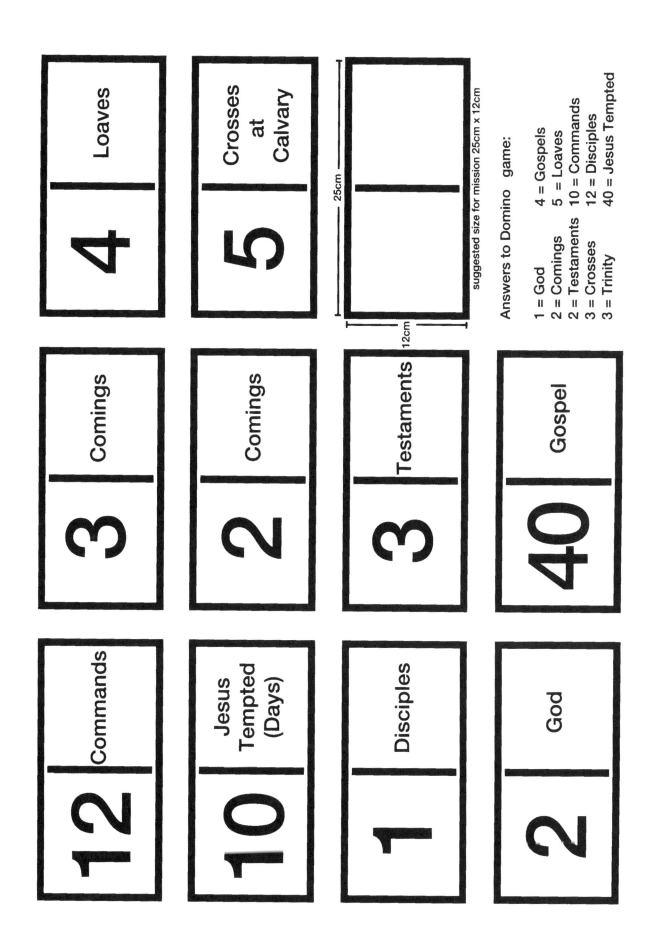

| 4 | Loaves |
| 5 | Crosses at Calvary |

3	Comings
2	Comings
3	Testaments
40	Gospel

12	Commands
10	Jesus Tempted (Days)
1	Disciples
2	God

25cm

12cm

suggested size for mission 25cm x 12cm

Answers to Domino game:

1 = God	4 = Gospels
2 = Comings	5 = Loaves
2 = Testaments	10 = Commands
3 = Crosses	12 = Disciples
3 = Trinity	40 = Jesus Tempted

21 Crown jewels

USES

This game is suitable for all ages. It is used to illustrate the fact that the Bible is like a torch, a map, a key and a sword and, as we get into it, we discover the 'crown jewels'.

EQUIPMENT NEEDED

- Passport cards (enough for each team), counters or markers,
- dice or a spinner,
- treasure map,
- suitable quiz questions.

HOW TO PLAY

It's counters and dice again!

The two teams work round the outer track, by answering questions alternately. Then they roll the dice or use the spinner to move their counter. As they land on a corner they collect a passport card (ie a key, a torch, a map or a sword).

When they have collected all four, they can enter the middle section of the track to claim the crown jewels, (which represent the kingdom of heaven).

The first team to the centre wins.

Two free choice squares give a free choice of passport cards.

Crown jewels

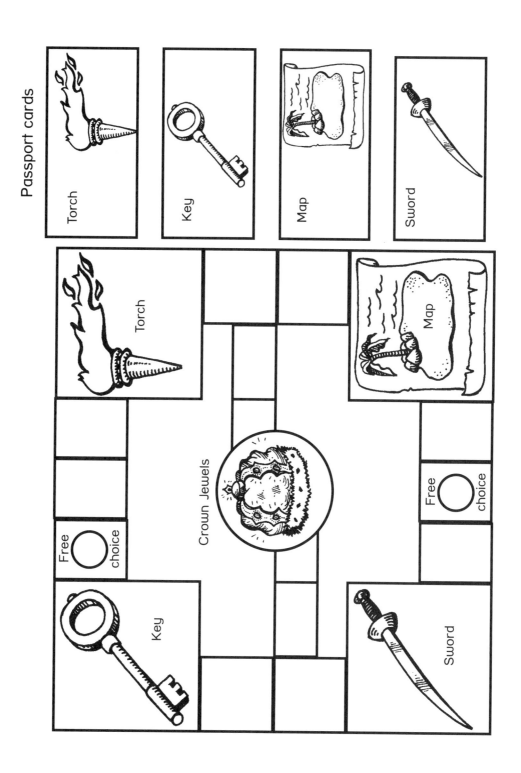

Passport cards

Torch

Key

Map

Sword

22 Criss-cross

USES

This game is a variation on noughts and crosses and is suitable for all ages and situations.

EQUIPMENT NEEDED

- Nine cards marked as shown in the illustration opposite and displayed on a grid,
- nine cards, marked with a cross on one side and a nought on the other, to cover each square,
- Velcro pads or adhesive tape to hold cards in place,
- a good supply of questions for each topic.

HOW TO PLAY

Teams choose a subject from the board. They are asked a question on that subject. If correct they place their team's symbol over the square. The first team to complete a row of noughts or crosses is the winner.

Other subjects can be substituted depending on the audience.

GOSPELS	TV	GEOGRAPHY
CHRISTMAS	GENERAL	EASTER
BOOKS	BIBLE BOOKS	NATURE

23 Three in a row

USES

This game is suitable for most situations and age ranges.

EQUIPMENT NEEDED

- A collection of circles with a different colour on either side, enough to fill the grid,
- a board marked as shown opposite, suitable quiz questions.

HOW TO PLAY

The object of the game is for one team to get three discs in a vertical, horizontal or diagonal row. Both teams are allocated a colour. Questions are asked of each team in turn. The person, who answers the question correctly, chooses the position on the board where they want to place the disc. They are then invited out to the front to do this for themselves. Their team mates can give them directions!

   Points per disc could be awarded, with bonus points added for a winning line.

   The game could be played against a time limit but the audience should be informed at the start.

Circle template	To fit inside squares	Three in a row		

24 Ludo

USES

This game is suitable for most events and activities, and is especially good for family services.

Because the game is generally well known and played at home, most children aged 5 and upwards will have a good understanding of how to play.

EQUIPMENT NEEDED

- Dice or a spinner to score with,
- large version of the playing board,
- counters for the team markers,
- suitable quiz questions.

HOW TO PLAY

The game is played as straightforward Ludo, but with only one counter per team. Questions are addressed to teams alternately, and if the answer is correct, counters are moved according to the dice or spinner score. The first team home wins.

The game can be used as an ongoing scoring system, used over several days or events. Make sure a careful note is made of the position of the counters at the end of each day, so that everyone is happy that there is no cheating.

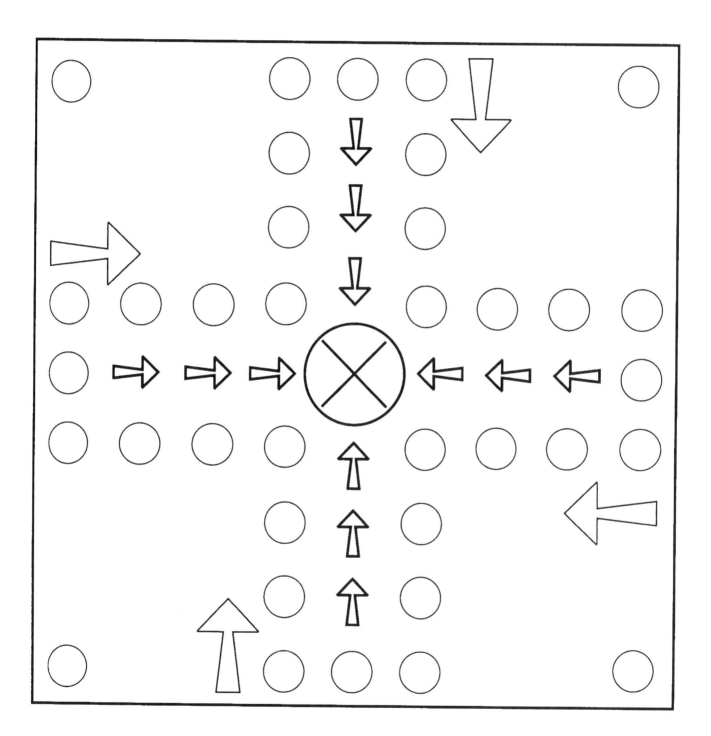

25 Battleships

USES

Here is a noisy version of the old favourite. 'Battleships' is especially good for the livelier situation.

Because of the noise, and type of game it is, it is really best for the 5 plus age group.

EQUIPMENT NEEDED

- Nine squares of card for each team (18 in total) coloured on one side and with either smiley suns [MISS] or explosions (HITS],
- a board to display them on, marked as shown in the illustration opposite,
- suitable quiz questions.

HOW TO PLAY

Cover each square of the grid with a card using one of the fixing methods mentioned earlier (see opposite). Make sure that the symbol on the card faces the board and not the audience.

Each side has an area of sea made up of nine squares. The object of the game is to find three 'hits'. Make sure that the 'hit' and 'miss' cards are in different positions on each board, otherwise the children will guess the positions very quickly. On answering a question correctly, the child gives a grid reference to indicate which square they have chosen.

If you use either magnetic tape or Velcro, put a piece on both sides of the card so that the pieces remain on the board and can be seen as a running score by the children and yourself.

To add more excitement, the children in the choosing team can make their own sound effects. Tell them what is allowed, perhaps they can shout, 'Bang!' for each 'hit', and, 'Phew!' for each 'miss'.

Make these from card.

18 cards needed in total. 9 each side.

3 hits are needed at least on each side.

Otherwise mix them up as you put them on to the board.

Hit cards

Miss cards

Make these from card.

18 cards needed in total. 9 each side.

3 hits are needed at least on each side.

Otherwise mix them up as you put them on to the board.

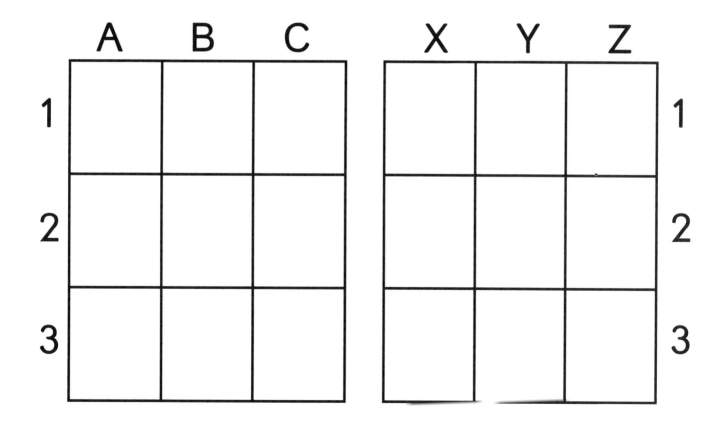

	A	B	C		X	Y	Z	
1								1
2								2
3								3

hit three ships to win

26 Shape shifters

USES

This game is based on a popular computer game. It is really only suitable for use in clubs and with groups of children.

It's a good game for children aged 5 plus, especially if you have a large number of children who play computer games.

EQUIPMENT NEEDED

- Eight shapes (templates for shapes shown opposite); giving each shape its own colour,
- A grid as shown in the illustration opposite,
- suitable quiz questions.
- Ensure that your version of the game board is made large enough for the venue.

HOW TO PLAY

Divide your group into two teams. Ask each team questions alternately. When a question is answered correctly, the person who answered it gives you a number: 1, 2, 3 or 4. Count through your pile of shapes until you reach the piece that is chosen by their number choice. This selects randomly their choice of shape. You then move it down from the top of the board following the directions of the child: left, right or down. The shape can be moved until it is at the bottom of the grid, or fitted against another shape already on the board.

Only the child answering the question correctly can give directions to the quiz leader as to the movement of the shape down the board.

The winning team is the one that completes a horizontal line across the grid.

Shape shifter grid

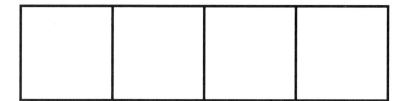

Shape shifters template

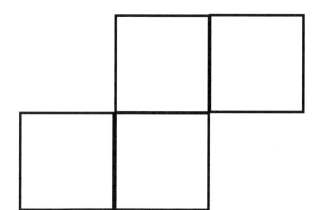

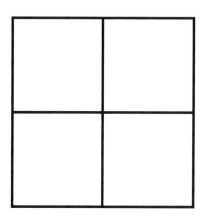

27 Quiz ball

This is a great quiz for those with a sporting interest, and useful for Missions and mid-week clubs.

It is suitable for 7- to 13-year-olds.

EQUIPMENT NEEDED

- Board as shown in the illustration opposite,
- football shape to move about the board,
- suitable quiz questions.

HOW TO PLAY

Divide your children into two teams. You could name them after local football teams. The aim of the game is to score a goal by answering five questions in succession.

Start the game with a general question to see who kicks off. If that team is unable to answer the question correctly, then the opposing team is offered the question. This can continue until a goal is scored, or, better still, against a time limit.

If neither team can answer a question, give a 'bounce' question open to both teams.

This is a fast-moving quiz with plenty of action across the board.

The game is won by the most goals, or declared a draw if no goals are scored.

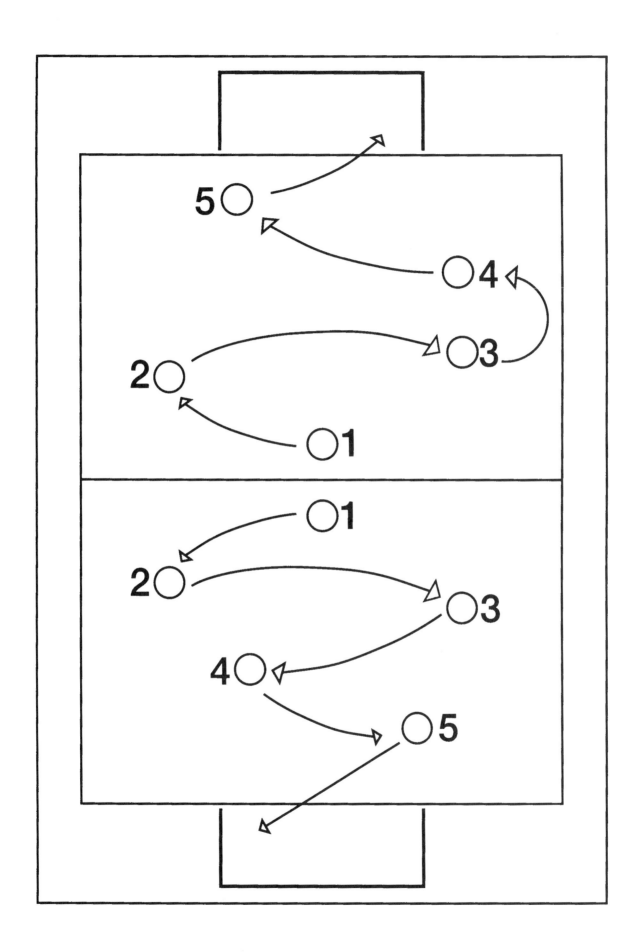

28 Space invaders

A game that needs to be played fast, based on a popular computer game. It is best used in mid-week clubs and Holiday clubs.

This quiz is best suited to 5- to 11-year-olds, who still enjoy playing this game.

EQUIPMENT NEEDED

- A computer screen board, as shown in the illustration opposite, sets of six cards – one set for each team – with the following words written on them:
- Hit 1 invader,
- Hit 2 invaders,
- Miss shelter,
- Hit shelter,
- Hit rocket base,
- Miss,
- a number of explosions drawn on cards,
- suitable quiz questions.

HOW TO PLAY

Ask questions to alternate teams. When a child answers correctly, they choose a card from the pile of six. This choice tells the team what they have done – hit or miss. You then use the explosion cards to cover those items on the board which are hit.

The first team to hit all four invaders is the winner. If a team hits both of its rocket bases then they have lost the game.

For added excitement, the children can shout, 'Kerpow!' when they score a hit.

Both boards are the same. Use the templates (opposite) to make space invaders, rocket bases and shelters. Remember to colour-code space invaders in green, rocket bases in red and shelters in white.

Space Invaders
(Template is needed for the invaders)

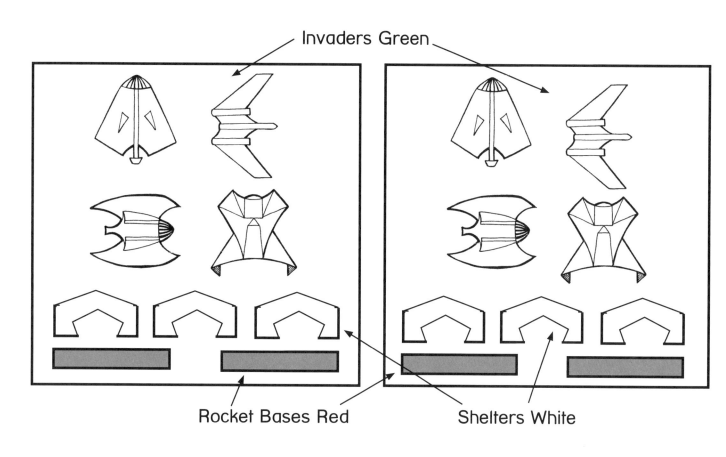

Invaders Green

Rocket Bases Red

Shelters White

Invaders Templates

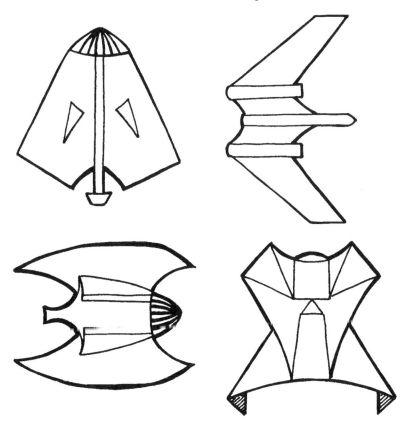

29 Snakes & ladders, two variations

USES

This well known and popular game is ideal for most events, with any age groupings.

There are many commercial board games that are easily adapted for this use. Some of these versions are fairly large and reasonably priced. Try one of the large toy shops.

EQUIPMENT NEEDED

- A version of the game, large enough to be seen from the back of your venue,
- Dice or spinner,
- team counters,
- suitable quiz questions.

HOW TO PLAY

Play this in the same way as the normal game of snakes and ladders.

The two variations in this book work on that same principle. Teams are asked questions alternately. When the answer is correct, the dice or spinner is used to obtain a score for the team counter to move up the ladders and down the snakes as normal.

You can of course alter this, but make sure the teams know which way they can move.

Depending on the number of teams taking part, you may wish to have a time limit on your quiz.

Don't go on too long, as the children will quickly lose interest.

The team furthest up the board at the end of the game is the winner.

For added effect, the children can be encouraged to cheer when they go up a ladder or groan, 'Aargh!' when they go down a snake.

The second variation is shown opposite.

This game is modelled on one produced in Tanzania a few years ago as an aid to general health education. This game features water supplies, and is a good way to learn something about the problems of getting clean water in some other parts of the world. (Remember, you go up the wells and down the drains!)

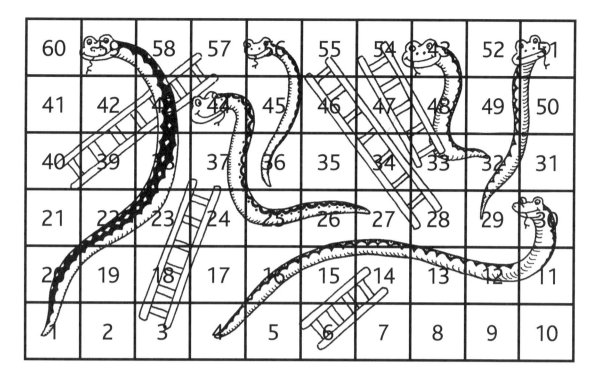

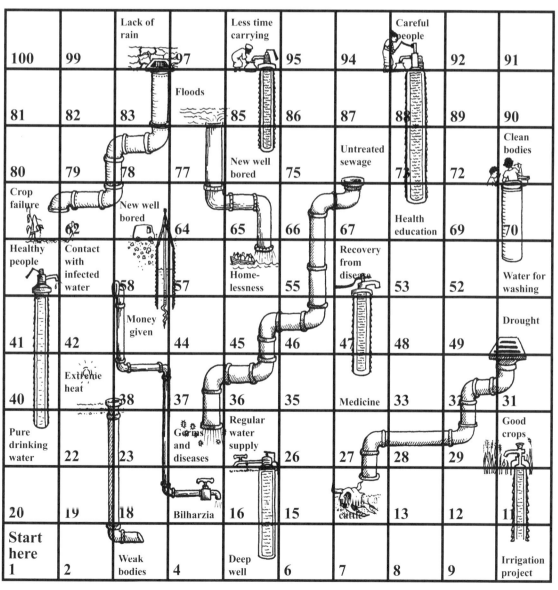

30 Ten pin bowling

USES

This is a variation on the skittles game, in this case, based on a board. It has been used on Beach Missions, and seems suitable for the 8-to13-year-old age group.

EQUIPMENT NEEDED

- Ten card skittles (see skittle template opposite) numbered 1 to 10 on the reverse,
- a board to display them, suitable quiz questions.

HOW TO PLAY

Arrange the skittles on the board, as shown in the illustration opposite. Mix them up so that they are randomly arranged.

Divide your group into two teams. Each team answers alternate questions. On answering correctly, that child chooses a skittle and the team score is on the reverse of their chosen skittle.

When all the skittles have been removed from the board, add up the score, and the team with the highest score is the winner.

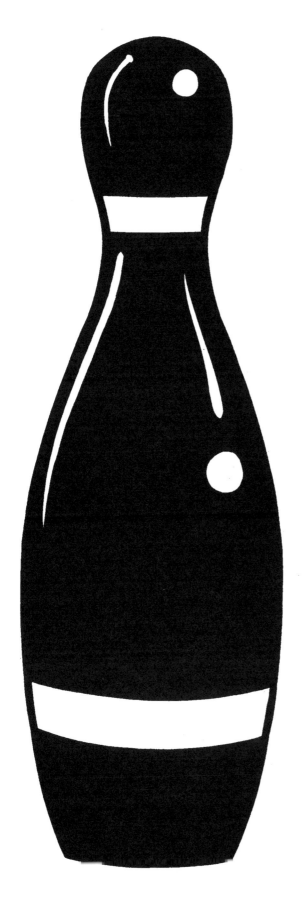

10 skittles numbered on
reverse 1 to 10

Arrange on your board in
the following pattern

31 Change 'em

A quiz based on the popular board game, but simplified to be used in a club situation. It only really works in mid-week clubs and Holiday clubs.

Because the game is a little complicated to understand at first, it is best for 8-year-olds and upwards.

- A board marked out as a grid made up of 16 squares (see illustration opposite),
- 16 circles of one colour with a different colour on the reverse side. Both sides of each circle will need either Velcro pad or a magnetic tape fixer,
- suitable quiz questions.

Divide your group into two teams. Give them a team colour. Ask questions alternately by team. The child answering correctly comes to the front, and aided by his team, places his coloured counter into any of the squares on the grid.

This continues with each team trying to capture the opposition's pieces. Opposition pieces can only be captured when the team blocks off a piece, or a row or diagonal, by having one piece of their team colour either side of the opposition's piece, row or diagonal.

For example:

1. First piece placed by the Red Team.
2. Second piece placed by the White Team.
3. Third piece placed by the Red Team. The Red Team wins the piece placed by the White Team. A member of the Red Team turns it over and so makes it a Red piece.

Thus, each team tries to win as many of the opponents' pieces over to their team colour as possible.

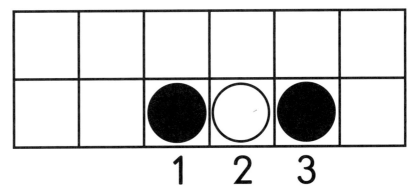

66

You may find that a time limit is the best way of completing this game, or the teams will spend too long considering where to place their piece on the board. A clue to success in this game is to go for the corner positions!

The winner is the team with the most colour pieces on the board at the end of the time limit, or questions.

Change 'em

16 circles, black one side white the other, or choose your own team colours.

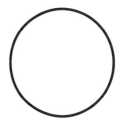

1	2	3	4
5	6	7	8
9	10	11	12
13	14	15	16

32 Munch 'em!

USES

This 'munch them up' board game can be used as a floor game as well.

It works best in mid-week and Holiday clubs and is suitable for most ages from 5 years old and upwards.

EQUIPMENT NEEDED

- Board marked out as shown opposite,
- dice or a spinner,
- two team shapes (see Munch 'em! templates below) of different colours,
- nine green squares, held on to the board by Velcro or magnetic tape; plain green on one side and with a monster on the reverse (see monster template below),
- suitable quiz questions.

HOW TO PLAY

Each team has a different coloured shape, which moves around the board getting green squares for its team. When a child answers a question correctly for its team, the roll of the dice decides the number of spots they can move. The child comes and moves its own team's shape the required number of spots, collecting any green squares it passes. The starting point for the whole game is in the middle of the board.

Note: on the back of the green squares are 'monsters'. These are collected in the squares either side of the board. Three is enough for your team to win.

On collecting the green square and the monster, the children can yell, 'Munch, gobble, gobble!'

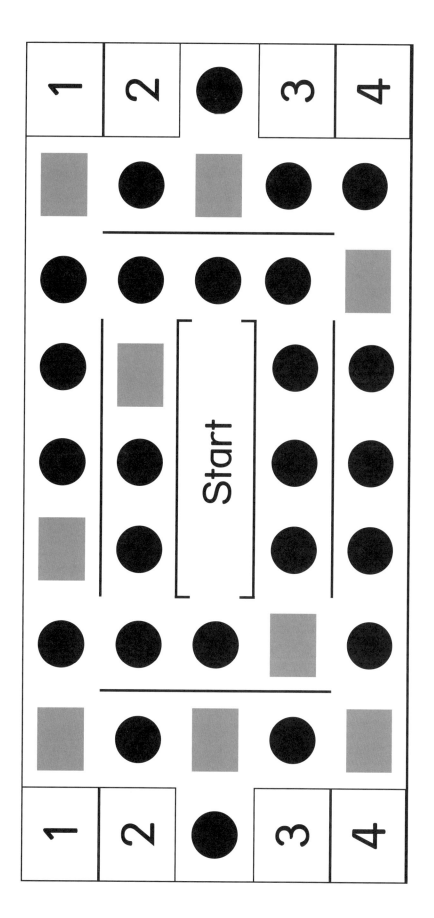

33 Go-do the journey

This game is similar to Monopoly and is suitable for use in small groups, or Holiday clubs and mid-week groups. The game was originally intended as a means of enabling people to share experiences together, and as a means of breaking down barriers and an aid to building relationships.

It really only works with children aged 8 plus, but works extremely well with most groups of young people and adults.

- An A3/A2 copy of the game board (see template opposite) for each group, which is big enough for all to see,
- a selection of cards, with things for people to 'go-do':
  for example, 'Go out of the room on two legs, and come back with six!'
[Answer: come back in with a chair.]
or, 'Go and stand on your own hands!' [Answer: not a hand stand.]
or, 'Say something nice to the person next to you!'
team counters,
dice or a spinner.

Roll the dice or a spinner to move your counter around the board, following the instructions in each square as you land on them.

If you land on 'Pick a Card', choose one from the top of the pile, and then do whatever the card instructs. (Do make sure that the cards are suitable for your group and situation.)

You can make up your own card details.

It is possible to create your own board based on local details or people, perhaps on what those taking part have been doing (see board template opposite).

When playing this game with small groups, it is possible to build in a move feature, so that the square could say, 'pick up your counter and move to the next group in the room'. This causes much hilarity, and helps people get to know a larger number of others in the room.

To make the game suitable as a quiz for two teams, the participants should answer questions correctly before rolling the dice, in order to move their counter.

Either set a time limit, in which case the team furthest around the board is the winner, or the winner is the first to reach square 40.

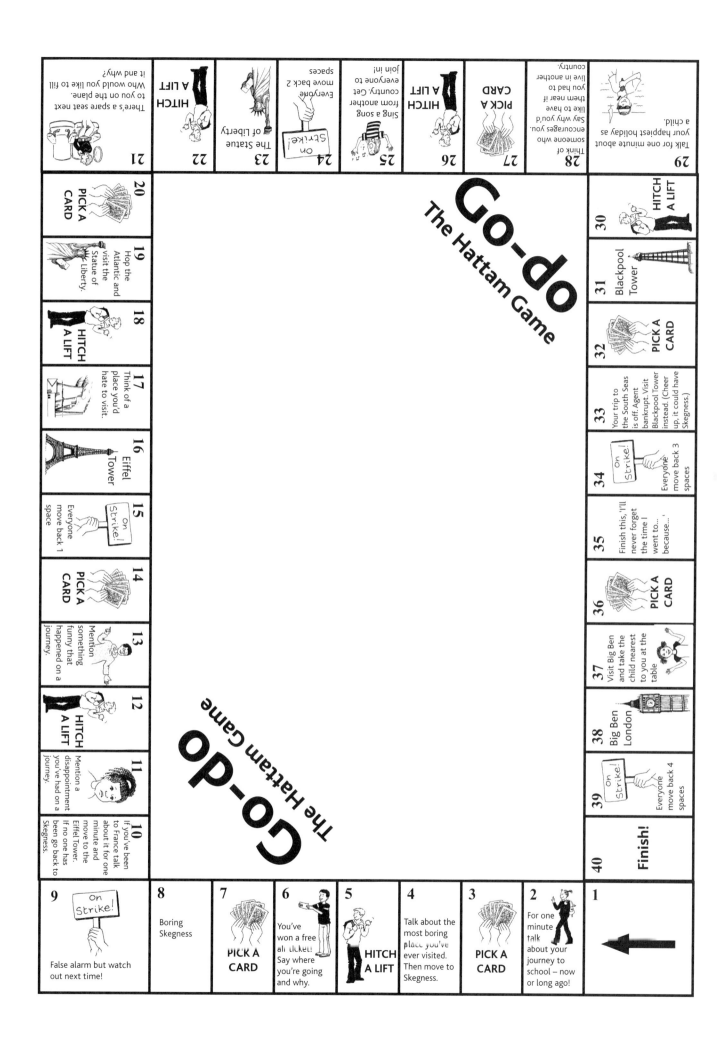

Go-do — The Hattam Game

21 There's a spare seat next to you on the plane. Who would you like to fill it and why?

22 HITCH A LIFT

23 The Statue of Liberty

24 On Strike! Everyone move back 2 spaces

25 Sing a song from another country. Get everyone to join in!

26 HITCH A LIFT

27 PICK A CARD

28 Think of someone who encourages you. Say why you'd like to have them near if you had to live in another country.

29 Talk for one minute about your happiest holiday as a child.

20 PICK A CARD

19 Hop the Atlantic and visit the Statue of Liberty.

18 HITCH A LIFT

17 Think of a place you'd hate to visit.

16 Eiffel Tower

15 On Strike! Everyone move back 1 space

14 PICK A CARD

13 Mention something funny that happened on a journey.

12 HITCH A LIFT

11 Mention a disappointment you've had on a journey.

10 If you've been to France talk about it for one minute and move to the Eiffel Tower. If no one has been go back to Skegness.

30 HITCH A LIFT

31 Blackpool Tower

32 PICK A CARD

33 Your trip to the South Seas is off. Agent bankrupt. Visit Blackpool Tower instead. (Cheer up, it could have been Skegness.)

34 On Strike! Everyone move back 3 spaces

35 Finish this, I'll never forget the time I went to… because…

36 PICK A CARD

37 Visit Big Ben and take the child nearest to you at the table

38 Big Ben London

39 On Strike! Everyone move back 4 spaces

40 Finish!

9 On Strike! False alarm but watch out next time!

8 Boring Skegness

7 PICK A CARD

6 You've won a free air ticket! Say where you're going and why.

5 HITCH A LIFT

4 Talk about the most boring place you've ever visited. Then move to Skegness.

3 PICK A CARD

2 For one minute talk about your journey to school – now or long ago!

1

34 Unwrap the parcel

USES

This is a variation on the old party favourite, 'pass the parcel'.

It is suitable for all ages, but is best used in a celebration type of service (Christmas, anniversary or birthday).

EQUIPMENT NEEDED

- A number of different sized boxes which will fit inside each other, wrapping paper,
- a selection of questions which need to be attached to each box as you prepare this quiz,
- a reward relating to the service theme may be contained in the last box to be opened (the first one to be wrapped),
- a general question to start the game off.

HOW TO PLAY

A general question is directed at the audience. The person with the correct answer is allowed to remove the first layer of wrapping paper, remove the box, and read the next question.

Questions may be directed at various age groups, ie under-10s, under-20s, grandparents, etc.

The game is over when the last box is unwrapped.

35 Cryptic clues

USES

This quiz is designed to test your understanding of the Bible. It requires a good deal of Bible knowledge*. It is best suited to those aged 14 and over.

It can be used by individuals competing against one another, or in small groups.

EQUIPMENT NEEDED

- Enough copies of the quiz for those taking part,
- if you have the use of an overhead projector, you may wish to prepare an acetate with the answers written on it,
- pencils to write with.

HOW TO PLAY

Quiz clues:
1   66 = B in the B [Answer: Books in the Bible.]
2   300 = L with their H to their M [Answer: Lapped with their Hands to their Mouths. See Judges 7:6.]
3   450 = L of the A [Answer: Length of the Ark. See Genesis 6:15.]
4   6 = D to make the W [Answer: Days to make the World. See Genesis 1:1 – 2:2.]
5   31 = P in the B [Answer: Proverbs (chapters) in the Bible.]
6   120 = P were waiting U [Answer: People were waiting Upstairs. See Acts 1:15.]
7   39 = B in the OT [Answer: Books in the Old Testament.]
8   12 = D who followed J [Answer: Disciples who followed Jesus. See Matthew 10:1–4.]
9   40 = D that M was on the M [Answer: Days that Moses was on the Mountain. See Exodus 24:18.]
10 12 = G in the HC [Answer: Gates in the Heavenly City. See Revelation 21:12.]
11 66 = C in I [Answer: Chapters in Isaiah.]
12 10 = P sent to the E [Answer: Plagues sent to the Egyptians. See Exodus 7:14 – 11:10]
13 350 = N after the F [Answer: Years Noah lived after the Flood. See Genesis 9:28.]
14 150 = P in the B [Answer: Psalms in the Bible.]
15 13 = T they circled J [Answer: Times they circled Jericho. See Joshua 6:8–16.]

* Answers based on the New International Version and Good News Bible translations.

36 Parables of the sower

USES

This quiz is suitable for any age.

EQUIPMENT NEEDED

- Copy this quiz on to an acetate sheet for use on an overhead projector,
- cut out some shapes to represent seeds, or use sunflower seeds,
- suitable quiz questions.

HOW TO PLAY

Divide your group into two teams, and ask questions to each team alternately. When a question is answered correctly, that person comes out and drops a seed on to the picture on the overhead projector. The score is as follows:

0 for landing on the pathway, weedy or stony ground;

the points as shown for landing on the good soil.

Another variation of this game is to draw it on to large sheets of card and lay it on the ground. Have several seeds cut from newspaper, so that they 'float' down when dropped. Score and play the game as in the instructions above.

WEEDY	30 GOOD SOIL	STONY	WEEDY	WEEDY
100 GOOD SOIL	WEEDY	60 GOOD SOIL	STONY	30 GOOD SOIL
WEEDY	STONY		WEEDY	STONY
STONY	100	STONY	WEEDY	60 GOOD SOIL
WEEDY	STONY	60 GOOD SOIL	STONY	WEEDY
STONY	30 GOOD SOIL	WEEDY	STONY	30 GOOD SOIL

PATHWAY

GOOD SOIL

37 Pick it

USES

This is a quiz for just about any age group and almost all situations. It is especially good for people with little or no Bible knowledge, as the answers are revealed and explained as the quiz progresses.

EQUIPMENT NEEDED

- A board to display the quiz on,
- nine cards with answers on one side and numbered from 1 to 9 on the other,
- a series of questions that relate to the answers.

HOW TO PLAY

Place the cards on the board (as shown below) with the answers face down and the numbers showing. Questions are asked alternately, team by team, eg 'Who was the mother of Jesus?' [Answer: 'Mary']. The answer given should be a number (this relates to one of the card numbers displayed, eg 5). The card numbered 5 is then uncovered to show the word written on the reverse side (eg Mary). If the answer is correct then the team scores one point and the card is removed from the board. If the answer is incorrect, the card is replaced on the board with the number showing. This continues until all the cards are chosen correctly. The quiz becomes a question of memory and knowledge. The winners are the team who uncover the most correct answers.

It is possible to play this game with people taking the place of the cards and speaking the answers.

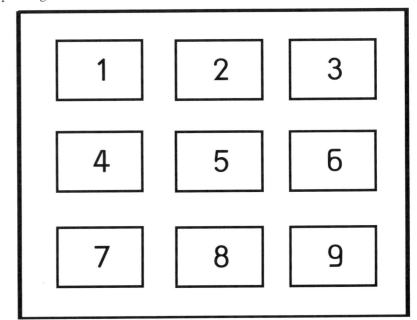

38 Find someone

USES

This quiz is best suited to an all-age occasion as a means of breaking down barriers and setting people at ease. It also starts people talking to one another.

EQUIPMENT NEEDED

- Copies of the quiz sheet for all those taking part,
- pencils to write with,
- suitable quiz questions.

HOW TO PLAY

The task, in the time allowed, is to 'find someone' who corresponds to each of the questions given, then to write their name against the question they match with.

Suggestions for questions

Find someone who:

1. has the same number of fillings as you do,
2. is the same age as you,
3. has a computer at home,
4. who hates the same TV programme as you,
5. who likes the same book as you,
6. who likes the same sport as you,
7. is wearing trainers,
8. is not wearing a watch,
9. has a cat for a pet,
10. drives a Volvo.

It is best to make your own set of questions that correspond to the group you are working with.

At the end of the quiz announce the winner.

39 Quiz relay

USES

A good quiz for all-age activities, but can be used for youth clubs and Holiday clubs. This quiz requires a large area, eg a school or church hall.

EQUIPMENT NEEDED

- A number of hoops or chairs – one for each team,
- suitable quiz questions.

HOW TO PLAY

Divide your group into teams. They can be arranged at one end of the room and at the other end place the hoops or chairs.

The teams compete together at answering the questions. When they think they have the correct answer, one team member runs to the hoop or chair for their team. The first one to reach it sits on the chair or stands in the hoop and the other teams' runners have to return to their teams. The quiz leader then asks for the answer from the person standing in the hoop or sitting on the chair. If they give a correct answer, their team scores points (eg 5 points for a correct answer). They then return to their team. If they give an incorrect answer, the other teams get a chance to run again. The quiz progresses like this until all the questions have been answered, or the time set for the quiz has expired.

The team with the most points at the end is the winner.

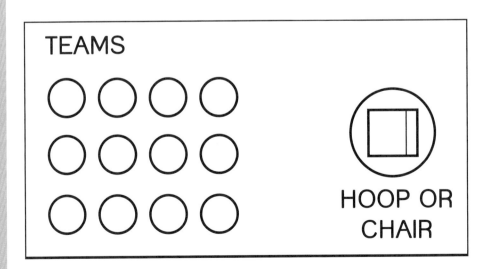

TEAMS

HOOP OR CHAIR

40 Jumpers

USES

This is a good quiz for all ages and situations if space allows – it requires a large area, eg a school or church hall. It is suitable for even the youngest of children.

EQUIPMENT NEEDED

- Questions for the teams to answer,
- a room or space big enough for those taking part,
- a finish line.

HOW TO PLAY

Divide your group into teams of equal numbers. Each team chooses a jumper (the person who will jump when their team gets the correct answers). They can only jump once for every correct answer their team gives. They must jump with both feet together. The team whose jumper is the first to reach the finish line, or is the nearest to the finish line, at the end of your questions (or set time) wins.

TEAMS

○ ○ ○ ○

○ ○ ○ ○   FINISH
                  LINE
○ ○ ○ ○

41 A-Z challenge

USES

This is a good all-age challenge, useful for making people feel at ease and to get them talking.

EQUIPMENT NEEDED

- Paper and pencils – enough for one of each per team.

HOW TO PLAY

Divide your group into teams. Each team writes the alphabet down one side of their piece of paper. The aim of the game is to match a Bible character to the letters of the alphabet.

For example:

A = Adam,

B = Bartholomew,

C = Cain, etc.

You could also use the same idea to set a challenge for other themes such as food/sport/cars or famous people.

The team with the most complete alphabet, in the time allowed, wins.

42 Mission impossible

This is a good quiz game for all ages to take part in. It is especially good for family events.

- A series of items written on to cards,
- paper and pencils.

Divide your group into teams of between six and ten people, of mixed age. Teams compete by sending a volunteer from each team to collect a card. The first volunteer has to act (mime) out the item from their card to their team. When the team has guessed correctly, the next volunteer has to get their team to guess the content of the next card by drawing a picture. The teams continue to alternate between mime and drawing until they have guessed all the items on the cards or reach the time limit for the quiz. The team that has guessed the most items correctly is the winner.

Examples of items that could be written on to the cards for teams to guess (remember to have some easier challenges for younger folk):

Acts 9:3–4 (Saul's encounter with Jesus),
Acts 3:6–8 (Peter and the crippled beggar),
John 6:11–13 (Jesus feeding the five thousand),
Matthew 7:24–25 (the wise man and the strong house),
John 11:43–45 (the raising of Lazarus).

The aim is to guess the characters or the teaching of the story. You could of course use all sorts of stories or items.

Ready to use quiz questions

The following series of quiz questions are designed to be examples of the different types you may wish to use. You will probably need to make some up yourself, to revise the teaching you have been doing, or to fit the service theme you are working on. Answers are based on the New International Version and Good News Bible translations.

True or False

True and false statements can be about any teaching from the Bible or about general knowledge. Worded properly, they are suitable for just about any age.
   Examples from the book of Jonah:
1   God asked Jonah to go to the city of Nivea?
     [Answer: false, it was Nineveh. See Jonah 1:2.]
2   Jonah ran away to Joppa?
     [Answer: true. See Jonah 1:3.]
3   Jonah was praying when the storm started?
     [Answer: false, he was asleep. See Jonah 1:6.]
4   Jonah was inside the fish for seven days?
     [Answer: false, he was inside the fish for three days and nights.
     See Jonah 1:17.]
5   Jonah did go to Nineveh?
     [Answer: true. See Jonah 3:3.]

Multiple choice

Think of different reasons for Bible events happening, and offer several possible alternatives as answers for the children to choose from.
   These questions take a bit of thinking about, and are probably best suited for children aged 8 plus.

1   Joseph's father gave him a present. Was it:
     a) a new pair of shoes, b) a new embroidered coat or
     c) a computer game? [Answer: b). See Genesis 37:3.]
2   When Moses saw the bush that was on fire, God told him to:
     a) take off his hat, b) take off his coat or c) take off his shoes?
     [Answer: c) See Exodus 3:5.]
3   When Zacchaeus could not see Jesus because of the crowd, he:
     a) used a pair of stilts, b) climbed a tree or c) flew in a helicopter?
     [Answer: b). See Luke 19:4.]

Who am I?

This type of quiz uses a series of clues to identify people or objects. Plan your clues so that the identity is not given away at the beginning.
   These types of question are best for children aged 8 plus.

1   a) I am a fisherman, b) My brother is called Andrew, c) Jesus healed my mother-in-law. [Answer: Peter. See Mark 1.]
2   a) I travelled with Paul, b) I was a doctor, c) I wrote a Gospel.

[Answer: Luke.]

3 a) I was a beauty queen, b) I was married to a king, c) I saved my people. [Answer: Esther. See the book of Esther.]

4 a) I am Joseph's younger brother, b) Silver was hidden in my sack, c) My father was called Jacob. [Answer: Benjamin. See Genesis 42–44.]

5 a) I am a short man. b) People didn't like me because of my job. c) I climbed a tree to see Jesus. [Answer: Zacchaeus. See Luke 19:1–10.]

6 a) 1 pretended to be my brother, b) I had 12 sons, c) One of my favourite sons was sold into slavery.
[Answer: Jacob. See Genesis 27,35,37.]

7 a) I was related to Jesus, b) I wore clothes made of camel hair, c) I baptised Jesus. [Answer: John the Baptist. See John 1.]

8 a) I walked with a limp, b) My father was Saul's son. c) King David was kind to me. [Answer: Mephibosheth. See 2 Samuel 4,9.]

9 a) I was a twin, b) I enjoyed hunting, c) I was known for being hairy! [Answer: Esau. See Genesis 25:24–27.]

10 a) I was a wealthy business woman, b) I dealt with purple cloth, c) I invited Paul to stay. [Answer: Lydia. See Acts 16:14–15.]

This quiz can be adapted to use local people like the vicar, the pastor or church administrator. Keep the clues straightforward and do not embarrass your victim.

You may wish to give points away depending on the number of clues used up before the correct answer is guessed.

Spot the mistake

Take a Bible narrative, preferably in a modern version and re-read it including a number of obvious errors. Because this type of quiz relies on some Bible knowledge, it is probably best suited for children aged 10 plus. Read the passage slowly, awarding a point for spotting the mistake and another for saying what it should have been.

Suggestion: the lost coin (Luke 15:8–10).

A woman who has six [ten] silver coins loses one of them – what does she do? She finds a torch [lights a lamp], gets out the Hoover [sweeps her house], and looks carefully everywhere until she finds it. When she finds it, she calls her friends and neighbours together, and says to them, 'I am so sad [happy]. I found the coin I lost. What an awful day [Let us celebrate!].'

Jumbled names or places

Make sure that the jumbled names or places will be familiar to those taking part. Names can be jumbled from the Bible, animals, pop groups, sports personalities, etc.

This style of question is best suited for an older age group.

For example:

ONIL = Lion,
REGTI = Tiger,
YRAM = Mary,
LAPU = Paul,
SUITT = Titus.

The individual letters can be drawn out on card, and then rearranged to give the correct answer.

Matching pairs

This game could use pairs of people from the Bible, the church or the television. If using local personalities, make sure they are well-known to your group.

This type of quiz question is suitable for all ages with the right choice of pairs!

1. Samson [Answer: and Delilah. See Judges 16:1–22.]
2. David [Answer: and Goliath. See 1 Samuel 17.]

3. Cain [Answer: and Abel. See Genesis 4:1–16.]
4. Mary [Answer: and Martha. See Luke 10:38–42.]
5. Tom and Jerry (cartoon characters).

Husbands and wives:
6. Adam [Answer: and Eve. See Genesis 3:20.]
7. Abraham [Answer: and Sarah. See Genesis 11:29.]
8. Isaac [Answer: and Rebekah. See Genesis 24:67.]
9. Ruth [Answer: and Boaz. See Ruth 4:13.]
10. Hannah [Answer: and Elkanah. See 1 Samuel 1:1–2.]
11. Mary [Answer: and Joseph. See Matthew 1:24.]
12. Ananias [Answer: and Sapphira. See Acts 5:1.]
13. Priscilla [Answer: and Aquila. See Acts 18:2.]
14. Zechariah [Answer: and Elizabeth. See Luke 1:5.]
15. Hosea [Answer: and Gomer. See Hosea 1:3.]

These can be written on to an acetate sheet, for use with an overhead projector, and the pairings joined with a line as the quiz progresses.

They could also be written on to cards and mixed up on a board; asking the group questions relating to a pairing; the answer being one of the pairs shown.

Fill in the missing word

This type of question and answer is especially useful for revision purposes.

It can teach a memory verse or be used as publicity for a special event, such as a barbecue or family service.

Suitable for older groups.

1. 'Everyone has _ _ _ _ _ _ and is far away from God's saving presence.'
[Answer: sinned. See Romans 3:23.]
2. Jesus answered, 'I am the way, the _ _ _ _ _, and the life.'
[Answer: truth. See John 14:6.]
3. The church picnic will be on _ _ _ _ _ _ _ _ at 3.30pm.
[Answer: Saturday.]
The statements should be written clearly either on cards or acetate sheets.

How many?

These quiz questions are suitable for children aged 7 plus.

1. How many loaves and fishes did Jesus use to feed the five thousand?
[Answer: 5 loaves and 2 fishes. See Matthew 14:13–21.]
2. How many commandments did God give to Moses?
[Answer: 10 commandments. See Exodus 20.]
3. How many tribes of Israel are there?
[Answer: 12 tribes. See Genesis 49:28.]
4. How many plagues did God send on Egypt?
[Answer: 10 plagues. See Exodus 7–13.]
5. How many of Joseph's brothers were sent to buy grain?
[Answer: 10 brothers. See Genesis 42:3.]
6. How many days was Jesus in the wilderness?
[Answer: 40 days. See Mark 1:13.]
7. How many days was Jonah in the fish?
[Answer: 3 days. See Jonah 1:17.]
8. How long did the flood last?
[Answer: 40 days. See Genesis 7:12.]
9. How many books in the Bible?
[Answer: 66 books in the whole Bible.]
10. How many coins had the woman lost in the story told by Jesus?

[Answer: 1 lost coin. See Luke 15:9.]

11. How many spies went in to Canaan?

[Answer: 12 spies. See Numbers 13:3–16.]

12. How many disciples did Jesus choose?

[Answer: 12 disciples. See Matthew 10:1.]

13. How many men did Gideon choose who lapped the water?

[Answer: 300 men lapped. See Judges 7:7.]

14. How many days did God take to create the world and everything in it?

[Answer: 6 days, on the seventh he rested. See Genesis 2:2.]

15. How many times did the Israelites march around the walls of Jericho on the last day, to make the walls fall?

[Answer: 7 times. See Joshua 6:15.]

16. How many friends came to talk with Job?

[Answer: 3 friends. See Job 2:11.]

17. How many sons did Noah have?

[Answer: 3 sons. See Genesis 6:10.]

18. How old was Josiah when he became king?

[Answer: 8 years old. See 2 Kings 22:1.]

19. How many churches have letters written to them in the book of Revelation?

[Answer: 7 churches. See Revelation 1:20

20. How many disciples were in the upper room?

[Answer: 11 were in the upper room. See Mark 16:14.]

Bible women

These quiz questions are suitable for children aged 7 plus.

1. Who was turned into a pillar of salt?

[Answer: Lot's wife. See Genesis 19:26.]

2. Who hung a red cord out of a window?

[Answer: Rahab. See Joshua 2:15–18.]

3. Who was the servant girl who answered the door to Peter after he was let out of prison?

[Answer: Rhoda. See Acts 12:13.]

4. Which woman in the Bible was a beauty queen?

[Answer: Esther. See Esther 2.]

5. Who was the great-grandmother of David?

[Answer: Ruth. See Ruth 4:13–22.]

6. Who was Isaac's wife?

[Answer: Rebekah. See Genesis 24.]

7. Whose husband worked 14 years for her?

[Answer: Rachel. See Genesis 29:16–30.]

8. Who was good with a needle, and was raised by Peter?

[Answer: Dorcas. See Acts 9:36–41.]

9. Who killed a general with a tent peg?

[Answer: Jael. See Judges 4:21.]

10. Who was Timothy's grandmother?

[Answer: Lois. See 2 Timothy 1:5.]

Relatives

These quiz questions are suitable for children aged 7 plus.

Guess the relationship of the following Bible characters:

1. Miriam and Aaron.

[Answer: brother and sister. See Numbers 26:59.]

2. Ruth and Orpah.

[Answer: sisters-in-law. See Ruth 1:14–15.]

3. Mordecai and Esther.

[Answer: cousins. See Esther 2:15.]

4. Hannah and Elkanah.

[Answer: husband and wife. See 1 Samuel 1:1–2.]
5. Esau and Jacob.
[Answer: twin brothers. See Genesis 25:24–26.]
6. Mary and Elizabeth.
[Answer: cousins*. See Luke 1:36.]
7. Saul and Jonathan.
[Answer: father and son. See 1 Samuel 13:16.]
8. Ananias and Sapphira.
[Answer: husband and wife. See Acts 5:1.]
9. Reuben and Benjamin.
[Answer: stepbrothers. See Genesis 35:23–24.]
10. Abraham and Jacob.
[Answer: grandfather and grandson. See 1 Chronicles 1:34.]

* Answer based on the Authorised Version translation

WHO?

These quiz questions are suitable for children aged 7 plus.
1. Who said, 'Let there be light'?
[Answer: God. See Genesis 1:3.]
2. Who said, 'Your people will be my people and your God my God'?
[Answer: Ruth. See Ruth 1:16.]
3. Which woman said, 'I am the Lord's servant'?
[Answer: Mary. See Luke 1:38.]
4. Who said, 'Go, sell everything you have and give to the poor'?
[Answer: Jesus. See Mark 10:21.]
5. Who was asked to build an ark from cypress wood?
[Answer: Noah. See Genesis 6:14.]
6. Who was asked to sacrifice his son?
[Answer: Abraham. See Genesis 22.]
7. Who stole his father's blessing?
[Answer: Jacob. See Genesis 27.]
8. Who was known as a hairy man?
[Answer: Esau. See Genesis 27.]
9. Who said, 'It would be better for me to die than to live,' while sitting under a vine?
[Answer: Jonah. See Jonah 4:8.]
10. Who was asked to go to the house on Straight Street?
[Answer: Ananias. See Acts 9:11.]

ANIMALS & BIRDS

These quiz questions are suitable for children aged 7 plus.

1. Which bird fed Elijah?
[Answer: ravens. See 1 Kings 17:6.]
2. Which bird did Noah send out of the Ark first?
[Answer: a raven. See Genesis 8:7.]
3. Which bird brought an olive leaf back to Noah?
|Answer: a dove. See Genesis 8:11.]
4. What kind of animal was Daniel imprisoned with?
[Answer: lions. See Daniel 6:16.]
5. In which creature's mouth did Peter find money to pay taxes?
[Answer: a fish. See Matthew 17:27.]
6. Which animal did Jesus ride into Jerusalem on?
[Answer: a donkey or colt. See Matthew 21:5.]
7. What creature did Moses make and put on a stick?
[Answer: a snake. See Numbers 21:8-9.]

8. Which animal was lost in Jesus' story?

[Answer: a sheep. See Matthew 18:10–14.]

9. Which animal spoke in the Bible?

[Answer: Balaam's donkey. See Numbers 22:22–35.]

10. Which creatures were the second plague on the Egyptians, when Moses was asking Pharaoh to let the people go?

[Answer: frogs. See Exodus 8:1–15.]

Which 'M'?

These quiz questions are suitable for 7 to 11s.

1. Which M saw a burning bush?

[Answer: Moses. See Exodus 3:2.]

2. Which M was the mother of Jesus?

[Answer: Mary. See Matthew 1:16.]

3. Which M had one brother and one sister?

[Answer: Martha. See John 11:1–3.]

4. Which M lived to be 969 years old?

[Answer: Methuselah. See Genesis 5:27.]

5. Which M worked for the Roman government?

[Answer: Matthew. See Matthew 9:9.]

6. Which M did God create on day six?

[Answer: man. See Genesis 1:26–31.]

7. Which M is the second Gospel?

[Answer: Mark.]

8. Which M was Esther's cousin?

[Answer: Mordecai. See Esther 2:15.]

9. Which M was a friend to Shadrach, Abednego and Belteshazzar (or Daniel)?

[Answer: Meshach. See Daniel 1:7.]

10. Which M was the sister of Moses?

[Answer: Miriam. See Numbers 26:59.]

Occupations

These quiz questions are suitable for 7 to 11s.

1. Was Peter:

a) a fisherman, b) a tax collector or c) a shepherd?

[Answer: A fisherman. See Matthew 4:18.]

2. Was Solomon:

a) a shepherd, b) a king or c) a slave?

[Answer: a king. See 1 Kings 2:12.]

3. What was Paul's job?

a) a gardener, b) a tent-maker or c) a tailor?

[Answer: a tent-maker. See Acts 18:3.]

4. What was Naaman?

a) a doctor, b) a disc jockey or c) a soldier?

[Answer: a soldier. See 2 Kings 5:1.]

5. What was Jonah?

a) a fisherman, b) a shepherd or c) a preacher?

[Answer: a preacher. See Jonah 1:2.]

6. Was Boaz:

a) a soldier, b) a farmer or c) a doctor?

[Answer: a farmer. See Ruth 2:3.]

7. Was Luke:

a) a fireman, b) a banker or c) a doctor?

[Answer: a doctor. See Colossians 4:14.]

8. Was Joseph (Jesus' adopted father):

a) a bricklayer, b) an architect or c) a carpenter?

[Answer: a carpenter. See Matthew 13:55.]

9. Did David the shepherd become:

a) a doctor, b) a king or c) a solicitor?
[Answer: a king. See 1 Samuel 16:1–13.]
10. Was Joseph asked to explain the king's:
a) choice of clothes, b) dreams or c) football results?
[Answer: his dreams. See Genesis 41.]

The following four sets of questions can be used to check the factual teaching of a passage of Scripture, or a particular Bible story. It would be sensible to include questions based on your story application. This would check that your group has understood the application of your teaching to their lives today.

These quiz questions are suitable for 7 to 11s.

The creation

1. In which book of the Bible do we first read of God creating the world?
[Answer: the book of Genesis.]
2. What did God create first?
[Answer: the heavens and the earth. See Genesis 1:1.]
3. According to the book of Genesis, on which day did God create the stars?
[Answer: the fourth day. See Genesis 1:14–19.]
4. What does Genesis say God did on the seventh day?
[Answer: he rested from his work and made it holy. See Genesis 2:1–3.]
5. What was the name of the garden God planted in the east?
[Answer: the garden of Eden. See Genesis 2:8.]
6. What trees grew in the middle of the garden of Eden?
[Answer: the tree of life and the tree of the knowledge of good and evil. See Genesis 2:9.]
7. What did God say would happen if the man ate of the tree of the knowledge of good and evil?
[Answer: the man would die. See Genesis 2:17.]
8. Who named all the animals God created?
[Answer: man. See Genesis 2:19–20.]
9. What did God take out of Adam to make the woman from?
[Answer: one of his ribs. See Genesis 2:22.]
10. Who tricked the man and woman into eating from the tree of the knowledge of good and evil?
[Answer: the serpent. See Genesis 3:4.]

Noah and the flood

1. Who found favour in the eyes of the Lord?
[Answer: Noah. See Genesis 6:8.]
2. Why was the Lord grieved?
[Answer: because of man's evil. See Genesis 6:5–6.]
3. How many sons did Noah have?
[Answer: three. See Genesis 6:10.]
4. Name the three sons of Noah.
[Answer: Shem, Ham and Japheth. See Genesis 6:10.]
5. What did God tell Noah to make?
[Answer: an ark. See Genesis 6:14.]
6. What wood did Noah make the ark from?
[Answer: cypress wood. See Genesis 6:14.]
7. How old was Noah when the flood came to the earth?
[Answer: 600 years old. See Genesis 7:6.]
8. How long did it rain ?
[Answer: 40 days and 40 nights. See Genesis 7:12.]
9. On which day of which month did the ark come to rest?

[Answer: on the 17th day of the seventh month. See Genesis 8:4.]
10. On which mountain did the ark come to rest?
[Answer: Mount Ararat. See Genesis 8:4.]

Moses and the burning bush

1. Whose flock was Moses tending?
[Answer: Jethro's – his father-in-law. See Exodus 3:1.]
2. What was Jethro's job/position?
[Answer: He was the priest of Midian. See Exodus 3:1.]
3. Where did Moses lead the flock?
[Answer: to the far side of the desert, to Horeb, the mountain of God. See Exodus 3:1.]
4. Who appeared to Moses at Horeb?
[Answer: the angel of the Lord. See Exodus 3:2.]
5. How did the angel appear to Moses?
[Answer: in flames of fire from within a bush. See Exodus 3:2.]
6. Who called to Moses from within the bush?
[Answer: God. See Exodus 3:4]
7. What did God tell Moses to take off?
[Answer: his sandals. See Exodus 3:5.]
8. Why did God say this to Moses?
[Answer: because Moses was standing on holy ground. See Exodus 3:5.]
9. Why did Moses hide his face?
[Answer: because he was afraid to look at God. See Exodus 3:6.]
10. What did God tell Moses he was going to do?
[Answer: rescue the people from the Egyptians. See Exodus 3:8.]

Gideon

1. Who spoke to Gideon under the oak tree in Ophrah?
[Answer: the angel of the lord. See Judges 6:11.]
2. What was Gideon told to do?
[Answer: save Israel out of Midian's hand. See Judges 6:14.]
3. What was the problem with Gideon's army?
[Answer: he had too many men. See Judges 7:2.]
4. How did Gideon choose the soldiers to go into battle with him?
[Answer: those who lapped water. See Judges 7:6–7.]
5. How many Midianites, Amalekites and their allies were there?
[Answer: they were as thick as locusts, their camels more than the sand on the seashore. See Judges 7:12.]
6. Who won the battle: Gideon and his 300 men or the Midianites, Amalekites and their allies?
[Answer: Gideon and his men. See Judges 7:22]
7. Who helped Gideon and his men?
[Answer: the Lord God. See Judges 7:22.]
8. Who did Gideon say would rule the land?
[Answer: the Lord. See Judges 8:23.]
9. What did Gideon make the gold earrings into?
[Answer: an ephod. See Judges 8:27.]
10. How long did Israel have peace during Gideon's lifetime?
[Answer: 40 years of peace. See Judges 8:28.]

ULTIMATE
Quizzes

Using the Ultimate series with your group

Whatever kind of group you run, a few extra ideas are always very much appreciated – even if you're following a printed programme. A printed programme will never fit your group exactly; there will always be activities that won't suit your veune, resources, skills or children's preferences. But don't despair! The producers of set programmes such as Light or a holiday club are happy for you to select and adapt the activities you need – actually they expect it!

So, what factors are likely to play a part in the activities you choose for your children?

The children

The children in your group should be the primary factor when choosing activities from the Ultimate series. You know your children best: how they learn, their characters, their interests and skills. If you have a chatty group, you might choose activities where the children can talk and discuss. If your group is quiet, you would probably steer clear of discussion activities, as too many of these may cause discomfort and unhappiness. However, it is good, at times, to challenge your group. Why not, once in a while, do a quiet, contemplative activity with a noisy group? Taking them gently outside their comfort zones means that they will experience something new and this will only serve to help them on their spiritual journey.

The skills of your team

The skills and talents of the team of leaders you have is another important factor to consider. If you have leaders with drama interests and abilities, then it would be good to make use of them. Similarly, talents for sport, art and craft, music or storytelling are great to use. Tailoring activities to leaders' skills and interests is also a good way to train your team in the skills needed to lead sessions.
If you don't have leaders with particular skills then don't do that kind of activity! For example, if you're running a holiday club and don't have dramatically minded leaders, then don't do the drama – it will only cause a lot of stress for the team involved!
The Ultimate series can help you fill in a leadership gap, giving you all the guidance you need to run craft or create visual aids, for example.

Resources

It would be wonderful if every church was bursting with coloured paper, sports equipment, sticky-backed plastic, data projectors and more. Unfortunately, money and resources (well, lack of them, to be more precise) is often an issue, and this will be another item for consideration when choosing your activities. You simply may not have the resources to do some activities. You should be able to find something in the Ultimate series to suit your requirements if you cannot do an activity suggested in a programme.
However, you may find that congregations respond very well to specific

requests for materials. A request for 4-pint milk cartons saw one craft expert almost buried by the number of plastic bottles he received. People tend to be more generous when they have a specific thing to collect or donate towards.

Venue

Almost no group has perfect surroundings, and so you'll have to do some compromising when it comes to space required for an activity. Be sensible about what you can do in your venue, and bear in mind the space restrictions placed on how many children you can fit into one room (at the time of going to press, the guidelines are 2.3 m^2 floor space per child). Be careful of hazards, and make sure you take steps to prevent injury. You may have to forego playing certain games if you have a small space, or refrain from cooking activities if you do not have the proper facilities. Again, the Ultimate series should provide extra ideas if you have to replace an activity because it does not fit your venue.

Your own preferences

These are, of course, important, as you don't want to be leading sessions which make you feel uncomfortable, but your own preferences should not be the main factor you use to choose activities. Try to push yourself and take on something you might not normally tackle. You may find that your group, and you, really engage with it!

ULTIMATE
Quizzes

Safety matters

Safety is important when playing those quizzes that involve a bit more activity. If you take the necessary precautions, you can play and learn in the most exciting way possible.

We work hard at preparing material and ideas for our groups; we pray about them, for them and with them – but how often do we think about the matter-of-fact safety aspects of working with children, young people and people of all ages? This is an article that, in one way, we hope you will never need. But at the same time, it is looking at areas of practical care that are just as important as spiritual nurture.

'But I haven't got time!'

'I can't do that as well as everything else!'

'I wouldn't know where to start!'

Don't worry – getting these things checked is not necessarily your job or your responsibility. But each of us needs to know that someone is doing these things – for the safety and well-being of those in our care and for our own safety too!

Case study exercise

Do this on your own or with a group.

'Can you give me some tips on keeping the children still?' she asked. 'We meet in the church kitchen where people make hot drinks. If the children run around, they will get hurt.'

What would you advise?

An initial reaction might be to say, 'Meet somewhere else!' But that isn't an answer which will help this children's leader. She is totally dedicated to the spiritual needs of her group – but somewhere along the line, she has lost sight of common sense and the most basic health and safety rules.

How would you answer the 'we meet in the kitchen' query?

What safety issues are involved?

What if it is the only space available for this group to meet?

Who has responsibility for the safety of the children in that group?

Risk assessment

In working on the case study, you have started to do a 'risk assessment', a process of thinking through the possible dangers or risks involved in a situation. It is not a precise science: it is a tool for you to use in assessing the risks involved. The process is important. You can use the risk assessment with other leaders, parents and carers to brainstorm the risks involved and to work together to identify hazards.

Why involve others?

• It helps all of you think through the safety issues.

• You are likely to identify more risks.

• It shares the workload.

Your final list may not be exhaustive but should include the obvious points.

Using a risk assessment method

Stage 1 Look for the hazards

A 'hazard' is anything that can cause harm.

These may include lifting heavy equipment, slippery floors, getting lost, blocked fire exits, water, stairs, using ladders, trailing power leads, poor lighting, lit candles.

Start your list with the potential everyday hazards involved in the activity or in using a particular room or area and then work through the risk(s) posed by that hazard. Start with the obvious.

Stage 2 Who is at risk?

A 'risk' is the chance, high or low, that someone may be harmed by the hazard.

Which groups of people or individuals might be affected?

Think especially about:
• anyone with disabilities;
• visitors or newcomers;
• inexperienced leaders;
• young children;
• groups meeting at a distance from the main site or building;
• whether any leaders are working alone with groups.

Stage 3 How well is the risk controlled?

Think through the risks involved.

For every hazard, there could be several risks. These may vary in probability and severity – and different people may have different opinions. Don't worry about that – it will be useful to air your ideas and discuss the possibilities: it will all add to your understanding of the safety issues. You may already be taking precautions to reduce the risk, but there is still likely to be some level of risk which may be high, medium or low. Your aim needs to be to make any risk as low as possible.

Consider:
• Are there legal requirements?
• What is good practice?
• Is there expert advice available?
• Can the risk be eliminated?
• Can the risk be controlled, so that harm is unlikely?
• Is there a less risky option?
• Can we do things differently or protect against the hazard?

If the risk is not already adequately controlled, go to Stage 4.

Stage 4 Record your decisions and what action is required

This is the critical bit! Think through a number of ways of improving the safety of the situation. You may decide to eliminate the risk by avoiding the hazard completely.

Stage 5 Review and revise

Have the measures you've planned or taken reduced the risk? Record the new level of risk here. As a team, decide if your changes are effective – and if not, go through the process again. You may need to follow up this assessment with other people in your church or organisation, maybe a minister, a caretaker or office staff. If you do identify a significant safety issue, don't assume someone else will notice: alert the appropriate person.

What next?

You can use this risk assessment method, for games and other aspects of your group, including:
- buildings and premises;
- fire;
- hygiene;
- health issues (including allergies);
- accidents and first aid provision;
- equipment (eg electrical, toys);
- individual activities that you are considering (eg taking a group of children out for a walk; cooking biscuits)

Many local councils, environmental health officers, fire and police services offer free advice on a range of health and safety matters: ask them and use them!

For first aid emergency advice, go to www.mothercare.com/stry/firstaidemergencies

For first aid emergency advice, training opportunities (including 'First aid for carers'), equipment and supplies find your national first aid organisation at www.orderofstjohn.org/frameset.htm (St John Ambulance) or www.ifrc.org/address/directory.asp (Red Cross directory).

UK readers can find a first aid course through
www.bbci.co.uk/health/firstaid
www.rospa.com
(Royal Society for the Prevention of Accidents) has invaluable advice on all aspects of safety education.
www.kidsafe.com.au
'Child safety is no accident' is the message from the Child Accident Prevention Foundation of Australia.
www.throughtheroof.org
Through the Roof offers specialist advice to churches and the wider society concerning disabled people and disability issues.
www.hse.gov.uk
Legal requirements and good practice information from the (UK) Health and Safety Executive.

Keep track of members of your group with a new style Wigmore register from www.scriptureunion.org.uk/shop

Other titles in the Ultimate Series:

Do you work with children or young people? Need that extra bit of inspiration to help your group explore the Bible? Want that extra idea to complete your session? Then the Ultimate series is for you! Each Ultimate book is packed full of ideas that have been used successfully by others and are more than likely to work for you!

Ultimate Craft

This book is crammed full of creative and imaginative ways to help you and your group explore the Bible through cutting, sticking, painting, drawing, sewing and, well, you get the idea! Inside you'll find all the instructions and guidance you need, together with helpful diagrams and photocopiable templates, so even the most craft-shy leader can make the most of this creative way to explore God's Word.
ISBN 978 1 84427 364 5
£12.99

Ultimate Games

This book is crammed full of creative and imaginative ways to help you and your group explore the Bible through playing games. Active games, quiet games, team games, individual games, games for children, games for young people – they're all here.
ISBN 978 1 84427 365 2
£9.99

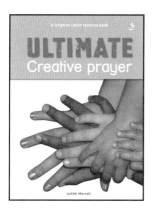

Ultimate Creative Prayer

This book is crammed full of creative and imaginative ways to help you and your group get praying. Ideas include prayers to draw and make, prayers to shout and sing, prayers to pray alone and pray together.
ISBN 978 1 84427 367 6
£9.99

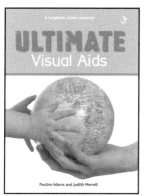

Ultimate Visual Aids

This CD-ROM is crammed full of creative and imaginative ways to help you and your group explore the Bible through using pictures. We all learn in different ways, and providing visual aids to illustrate the Bible will help visual learners really get into the story.
ISBN 978 1 84427 355 3
£9.99

Index

Quiz presentation ideas

Ready-to-use quiz questions